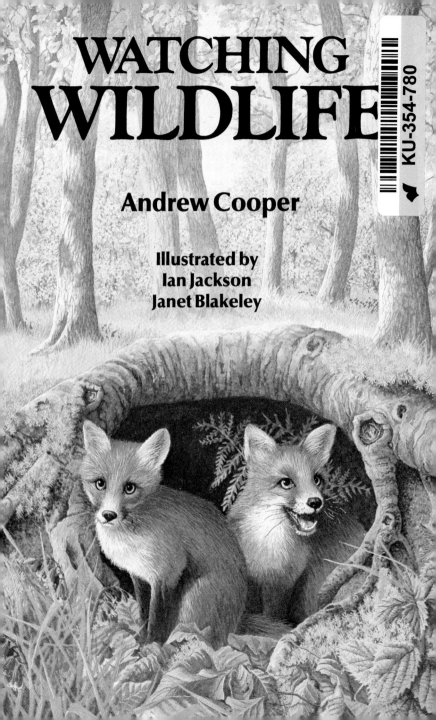

WATCHING WILDLIFE

Andrew Cooper

**Illustrated by
Ian Jackson
Janet Blakeley**

CONTENTS

Edited by Martyn Bramwell
Designed by Caroline Hill

Additional illustrations by Alan Harris, John Sibbick, David Hurrell/Middletons
Photographs by David Ridge, Michael Chinery and Geoffrey Kinns
The editor wishes to thank David Beeson and YHA Services Ltd. for their
help in preparing this book.

First published in 1982 by Usborne Publishing Limited,
20 Garrick Street, London WC2E 9BJ

Made and Printed in Great Britain
by Blantyre Printing and Bookbinding Ltd., London and Glasgow.

INTRODUCTION

This book provides the basics of where, when, and how to watch animals in the wild. It shows how, with a little effort, you can experience the natural world at first hand, by relearning how to detect and observe mammals, birds, reptiles, amphibians, and small invertebrates, such as insects and spiders. The skills that were second nature to our ancestors can be reawakened, and used to open up a fascinating new world that begins right on your own doorstep.

The first few sections of the book describe the techniques of locating the animals, then tracking or attracting them, and getting in close to watch them. They explain what you should take with you, and why, and provide a wealth of practical information on observing, understanding, photographing and recording what you see. Projects throughout the book will challenge your skills and shed new light on the hidden worlds around us.

Later sections of the book describe the habits and habitats of many of the animals you are likely to see, with further tips on how best to observe them.

Once the basics of fieldcraft have been mastered, more detailed field guides and handbooks will be useful to you; a brief selection is listed on page 62. If you wish to develop your skills further, you can seek help and advice from members of the various wildlife societies and clubs, also listed on page 62.

The naturalist's code
The "golden rule" of watching wildlife is that the animal's welfare comes first. Anyone can blunder about and perhaps catch a fleeting glimpse of a fleeing animal but it takes skill, understanding and patience to observe without being detected. It takes practice, but the rewards are huge. Good fieldcraft might well be repaid by the sight of fox cubs wrestling by moonlight, by the "plop" of a water vole diving into a stream, or by the sight and sound of a red deer stag bellowing his challenge to all comers.

▼ A well-positioned observer is rewarded for his skill and patience as the fox closes in.

TECHNIQUES OF FIELDCRAFT

A battle of wits

All animals have a powerful instinct for survival. Their senses are ever alert to danger and while some rely on camouflage to protect them, others rely on speed to make their escape. Their tolerance of man, however, is very variable and this makes some species much easier to observe than others.

Many birds and insects are quite easy to approach and observe. Mammals are by far the most difficult – but also the most rewarding. It is an exciting challenge to pit your wits and knowledge against an animal's survival instinct and acute senses, and the main ingredients for success are stealth, cunning, patience and preparation – including a well-thought-out plan. While our eyesight and hearing are as good as those of some animals, they come a poor second to those of many more. As for our sense of smell, it barely exists. We cannot even imagine its sensitivity in animals like the fox or deer. (Who are we to say the fox is a smelly animal? We can smell him at thirty yards, but he can smell us at half a mile or more!)

Generations ago we lost the need to use our senses instinctively but with a little practice we can retune them to life in the wild, even though we can never hope to match those of the animals we seek.

Moving through woodland

Movement will betray your presence to everything from a butterfly to a badger, so learning how to remain still is as important as learning how to move with the minimum of noise. One of the best ways to see wildlife is to choose a likely spot in a wood and then sit perfectly still, with your back against a tree (see below). After a while the animals will emerge and go about their normal business; you will see far more than on a dozen

▼ By keeping quiet and still this observer has become "part of the background" and will be ignored by the woodland wildlife until she stands up or makes a careless movement.

Treecreeper

Great spotted woodpecker

Nuthatch

Roe deer

Squirrel

4

Woodpigeons

Rabbits

▲ When out walking, keep a sharp lookout for woodpigeons, jays or crows and avoid them if possible. All are superb sentries, and woodpigeons in particular will "explode" from their tree with a tremendous din at your approach – sending every other animal straight into hiding.

walks through the same area.

When you *do* walk, keep to damp grass, avoiding dry leaves and twigs. The crack of a dry twig is about the quickest way known of sending everything into hiding. If you use a path regularly, make a habit of removing such tell-tales – especially near a badger sett or bird's nest. To walk silently on leaves for short distances, wear soft shoes and at each step gently move your foot from side to side to clear the leaves out of the way. If you have to walk through leaves for a longer distance it is better to slide the feet – making a soft continuous noise rather than a loud intermittent one. Remember that damp vegetation is always less noisy than dry, so walks after rain, or with morning dew still on the ground, are often the most fruitful.

Riverbank and marsh

Always try to "read" the landscape and plan your route for concealment and quietness. On the riverbank try to walk on grass or sand, avoiding noisy shingle and clinking stones. If you need to climb the bank, do so where you can climb smoothly and safely, without dislodging an avalanche of earth, and if possible where bushes will give cover as you reach the top.

When moving through reeds, wait for them to sway in the breeze and move with them, stopping again as each gust dies away. The same applies in any long vegetation. If you fit your own movements to any natural rhythms you will be rather less conspicuous.

In open country

When you are stalking animals in open country, wind direction takes on even greater importance. Check constantly and change your route as often as necessary to keep you down-wind of the animals. Move steadily, stopping frequently to look and listen, and above all do not talk. Try to keep your subject in sight and learn from its reactions. If startled it will flee; if just suspicious it will remain quite still until satisfied that it was a "false alarm". If possible, stalk animals when they are feeding or otherwise engaged, but remain alert and "freeze" the second an animal looks in your direction. Move again when it has resumed its activities – and when nearby animals have ceased to show concern.

5

The art of concealment

Camouflage is a very effective means of concealment that uses colour, pattern and texture to break up the tell-tale outline of an animal's body and help it blend in with its natural background. It can take many forms, from the elaborate disguises of many insects to the sand-speckled colouring of a flatfish and the delicately marked coat of a young fawn that merges so well with the light-dappled floor of the forest (see opposite). Some animals have this protection only when young and vulnerable; others, like the remarkable bittern of our reedbeds, are protected in adult life. Some creatures, like the Arctic fox, the stoat and the ptarmigan, change their colouring according to the season; but the picture of the stoat opposite shows what happens when this change is not quite fast enough!

▲ Concealed by his drab clothing, his boulder-strewn position, and by the dark hillside behind him, this naturalist watches deer feeding on the slopes below. Only the sun glinting on his binoculars, or an unlucky shift in wind direction, is likely to cause him any problem.

By studying animal camouflage we too can learn the art of concealment. The first principle, however, is to remain still – for any movement will destroy the effectiveness of even the best camouflage.

Wear subdued colours that blend with the landscape. Dull browns and greens are good, but better still is the irregular disruptive patterning used on military camouflage jackets. This breaks up the symmetrical outline of the figure. The giveaway human outline can also be disguised against natural shapes. By sitting crouched among boulders on a hillside you become part of the outcrop; by standing with your back to a tree you again break up your shape. A hat or anorak hood will hide a shiny forehead and for very wary subjects the face can be darkened with smears of earth or be covered

▲ Full of enthusiasm but doomed to disappointment, talkative walkers stride over the brow of a hill. The local wildlife will have taken cover long before they arrive. The colourful jacket, excellent in bad weather or an emergency, would be better carried in the back-pack until needed.

by a veil of dark netting. (Even for animals one of the biggest problems is to hide the glint of the eye.) But remember that none of this will work if you wear loose wellingtons that make a slapping sound, or if you have loose change jangling in your pocket.

Use natural cover at every opportunity but don't be tempted to fix leaves and twigs to your clothes. They rustle and shake at every slight movement and will frighten away every creature within earshot.

Keeping your head down

Remember that nothing will put an animal to flight faster than the sudden appearance of a human silhouette on the skyline. Keep below the brow of a hill; always look under, through, or round a hedge rather than over the top; and bear in mind that most of the animals you seek see the world virtually from ground level – it is *their* skyline you must beware of. If you have to crawl along the ground to get closer to your subject, use every bit of natural cover. Even the shallowest depression in the ground will completely hide you from an animal whose eye is only a few inches above the ground; nevertheless be very careful when you raise your head.

Breaking cover

Sometimes it is necessary to leave your cover but you can reduce the impact of your silhouette if you keep some cover, a hillside or wood, behind you. Always look carefully before stepping out of cover and never walk straight through a gateway or a gap in a hedge. Instead, peer round the edge first.

Lessons from nature

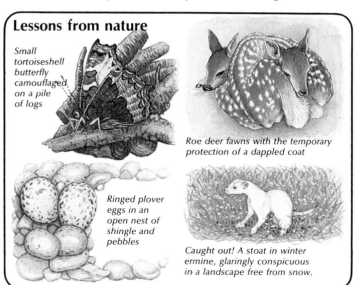

Small tortoiseshell butterfly camouflaged on a pile of logs

Roe deer fawns with the temporary protection of a dappled coat

Ringed plover eggs in an open nest of shingle and pebbles

Caught out! A stoat in winter ermine, glaringly conspicuous in a landscape free from snow.

Reading the signs

One of the most satisfying of all fieldcraft skills is the ability to read the subtle signs left by birds, insects and mammals as they go about their everyday lives. To the novice these signs are often very difficult to see but with practice they can be recognized quite readily and can add a new dimension to watching animals.

The most obvious signs are the tracks left by ground-dwelling animals and these are most clearly visible when made in a thin layer of fresh snow, in damp sand, or in soft, slightly muddy, ground. The best way to learn the various footmarks is to make careful drawings, to scale, each time you find one. You can also make casts of animal tracks using plaster of Paris poured into a retaining ring of card or metal pressed into the earth around the print. At some point you may even have the good fortune to come across the tell-tale marks of some natural drama: the tiny footprints of a mouse ending abruptly in disturbed snow showing the marks of an owl's feathers, or the scattered remains of a vole's nest left by a marauding fox.

But there is much more to the silent "language" of signs than just footprints. Vegetation of all types, from turnips to hazelnuts, pine cones to dandelions, may carry the marks of feeding animals – each one leaving its characteristic "signature" in the shape of the teeth marks, the part of the plant taken, the debris left behind, and the method of attack. Many animals and birds have favourite feeding places which may be littered with nut shells or splintered cones; birds in particular commonly wedge nuts or cones into bark crevices in order to peck at them, and again each species leaves

Bird pellet analysis

Measure the size of the pellet and note its shape. Then soak it and gently separate and identify the contents.

Common gull ▶
Up to 8cm long and 2cm in diameter. Variable content: fish bones, plant fibre and husks, insect remains.

◀ Sparrowhawk
Between 2 and 4cm long, about 1.5cm in diameter. Very firm and compact; made up mainly of mammal fur and small feathers.

its own "signature".

As animals eat, so they must get rid of bodily waste, and animal droppings can provide a fascinating source of information on what the resident animals have been eating. A great many birds pass only fluid waste in their droppings and retain the hard parts of ther diet (bits of shell, bones, insect wing-cases, grit and so on) which are then regurgitated from the crop in the form of a compact little bundle, or pellet (see above). These can be collected and broken open to reveal what the owl, or gull, or rook has been feeding on.

Once you become accustomed to tracks, feeding signs, territorial boundary marks and so on you will find yourself more and more adept at locating various animals' favourite routes and will therefore be able to track them more easily.

Tree damage

Larch attacked ▶
by black wood-
pecker after ants

Tree
brought
down by
a beaver ▶

Young conifer
stripped by
bank vole ▼

Nuts and cones

Spruce cone gnawed ▲
to core by a mouse

Woodpecker's
"workshop" ▶

Hazelnut
neatly emptied
by a wood
mouse ▼

Scent marking

To mark his
territory the
roebuck has
rubbed his
forehead gland
on a young tree,
damaging the
tender bark with
his antlers

Droppings

▲ *Fox*

▼*Fallow deer*

▲ *Badger's*
dung pit
latrine or

Fruits, stems and roots

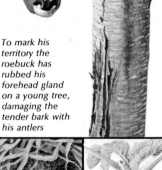

▲ *Apples*
damaged by
crossbills

◀ *Turnip gnawed*
away by hares
or rabbits

▼ *Rushes nibbled*
by field voles

Getting in close

Once you are familiar with the basic ideas of camouflage, and using cover to disguise your movements, you can get down to the exciting business of getting in close to your subject. And that is when every trick of fieldcraft will be important. But don't be discouraged if insects fly off, or if rabbits bolt down their holes while you are still some way off. It takes time and practice to develop really good fieldcraft.

Try to remember always that while we watch animals for pleasure, animals watch each other (and man in particular) for far more serious reasons. Any large and unfamiliar shape, any strange sound, and especially any "foreign" scent, spells *Danger!* to a wild animal. This does not always mean, however, that the animal will bolt. Sometimes animals can be right under your feet, but so well concealed that you may not spot them. Learn to expect the unexpected – you may be surprised by what turns up!

For example, last summer I was filming in Jersey and had spent almost a whole day, very hot and very frustrated, looking for green lizards. Not one was to be seen. I contented myself filming some wild flowers and was walking back across the sand between thick tussocks of grass, when a metallic scraping sound caught my attention. At my feet was an old beer can. Two tiny eyes peered from the "keyhole" opening and my suspicions were soon confirmed by the flickering of a forked tongue and the flash of brilliant green scales. After a pause a beautiful green lizard the length of my foot emerged into the sunshine, blinked for a moment or two, and then scurried off, just like some brilliantly-jewelled mechanical toy.

Normally, of course, you will have to use all the skills of fieldcraft to get so close to an animal. The following hints and tips may be of use.

Green lizard (male)

▲ Many animals can squeeze through surprisingly small openings.

Using an ash bag

A wet finger held aloft, or a light piece of grass tossed in the air, might tell you the wind direction when a gentle breeze is blowing, but even the lightest movement of air will carry your scent far and wide. So how are you to plan your stalk when you can't feel any wind?

The answer is to make an ash bag: a simple cotton bag, closed by a draw-string and filled with fine wood ash. To test the wind just flick the bag with a finger. The puff of ash will drift in the air and reveal even the slightest movement. The trick was devised many years ago by hunters in Africa: today we can put it to more peaceful purposes.

The benefits of snowfall

A thin, even, fall of snow is a great bonus to the wildlife watcher. Get out into the country near your home just as soon as possible and locate

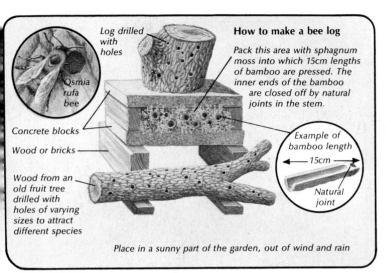

How to make a bee log

Pack this area with sphagnum moss into which 15cm lengths of bamboo are pressed. The inner ends of the bamboo are closed off by natural joints in the stem.

Log drilled with holes

Osmia rufa bee

Concrete blocks

Wood or bricks

Wood from an old fruit tree drilled with holes of varying sizes to attract different species

Example of bamboo length

← 15cm →

Natural joint

Place in a sunny part of the garden, out of wind and rain

and identify as many animal tracks as you can. Make notes of where the trails cross the roads, where they pass through gates or gaps in hedges, and note where any animal has stopped to investigate something or to leave a scent mark.

All this information can be plotted on a sketch map, perhaps using colours for the different animals. Then, when the snow has gone, you will know just where to look for the tracks and very often you will also know exactly where the nest or burrow is so you will have ample time to plan a good observation position before the breeding season starts.

Make practice a habit

"Practice" sounds too much like homework, so make a game of it. If you are in a park, or out for a walk, try setting yourself puzzles. Pick a spot at the far side of a small valley, or across the local park or playing field. If there are feeding birds, or squirrels, between you and the target, so much the better. Then plan a route to the target using every scrap of available cover, assuming first that the wind is from your left, then from your right, from in front and from behind you. Whenever there is time, actually do the stalk – seeing how close to the birds or squirrels you can get before they scatter.

Attracting wildlife to you

One way of ensuring that you get close to an animal is to attract it to you in some way, either by baiting (see pages 24–5) or, as shown above, by providing it with suitable materials for making a home. A selection of ready-made nesting sites in a "bee log" will encourage solitary bees and wasps to nest in your garden, where you can then watch them.

Knowing when to leave

▼ Red deer stag roaring in rut with unconcerned hinds grazing nearby.

Although getting in close will be one of your main objectives, the true naturalist is always aware of the fact that he is an intruder and that his presence can have a marked effect on the behaviour of many animals. Learn to recognize the warning signs so that by knowing when to withdraw you will avoid doing any harm to the wildlife you wish to study.

In some situations (luckily not many) such knowledge may save you being on the receiving end of a sharp reminder of what is, and what is not, good fieldcraft. For example, it should go without saying that you never put your hand down a burrow unless you know for sure that it is unoccupied. Ignore that rule and you are asking to get your fingers badly bitten, stung or pecked (puffins make burrows too!)

Season of aggression

The ritualized combat of red deer in rut can be a spectacular sight but at the height of the autumn rutting (breeding) season the stags can be very unpredictable. More than one person has been charged after approaching too close – presumably having been taken as a potential rival by a stag vigorously defending his leadership of a herd of hinds. The alarm signal is a series of sharp barks, while suspicion is shown by the stag holding his head high while raising and lowering the forelegs in a slow, stiff, "high-stepping" motion.

Some of our larger birds can also be dangerous if approached on the nest. Swans and geese in particular can deliver a fierce attack so it is always wise to drop back if a sitting bird shows signs of agitation. It is also illegal to "wilfully disturb" most species of birds, so *never* approach a nest except in the company of an experienced, authorized bird-watcher.

◀ Alpine marmot sitting upright in sentry posture with others feeding nearby.

Social warnings

Many of the social mammals, and also many birds, post "sentries" while the majority are feeding. The European marmot is a typical example: a shrill whistle from a lookout will send the entire colony underground in a flash and even the Alpine chamois will react to the marmot's alarm signal.

The rabbit has a dual alarm system. An individual sensing danger will beat its hind feet on the ground to alert the others; the signal is reinforced by the flashing of the white tail as the rabbit runs for cover.

◀ Toad inflated to put off attack by grass snake.

Desperate measures

Extreme agitation can produce very unusual and apparently bizarre behaviour in some animals. Toads will react to threat by arching the back and throwing up the head, often inflating the body in an attempt to discourage the attacker. If handled roughly, the grass snake goes one better, twisting onto its back and lying quite still with its mouth agape in imitation of death.

Nesting birds in particular have a number of marked behaviour patterns indicating distress and these must be heeded *immediately*. If a parent bird is prevented from getting back to the nest it may become so distraught that it abandons the nest entirely – with the loss of the eggs or nestlings. Agitation may be shown by the bird darting back and forth with high-pitched cries or by more elaborate behaviour. A bird that remains nearby, continually preening itself, while you are watching the nest, is becoming increasingly agitated and you should withdraw immediately. More elabo-

Plover's broken ▶ wing trick.

rate still is the ploy used by a number of ground-nesting birds. The ptarmigan will defend its nest bravely and even if a chick is seized the parent will not flee but will beat the ground and feign a wing-injury in an effort to lure the attacker away to an apparently "easy" victim. The shore-nesting ringed plover is another superb exponent of the "broken wing" trick.

The fact that an animal is alarmed does not automatically mean an end to the day's watching; a temporary withdrawal may be all that is required. Recognizing the signs that an animal knows you are there may perhaps enable you to keep it in view all afternoon instead of seeing it take fright and disappear.

OBSERVING AND RECORDING

What to carry

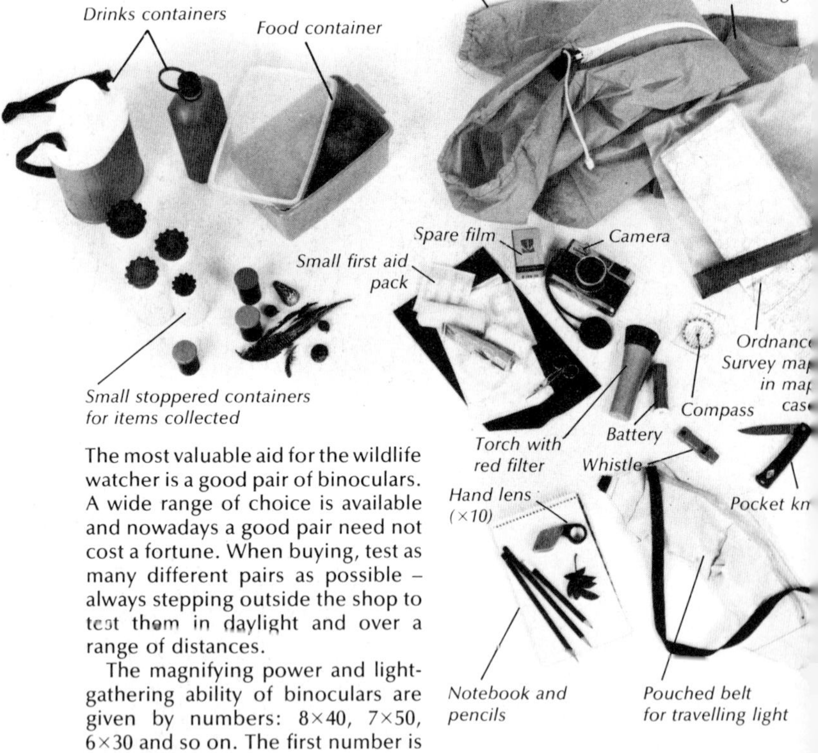

Conspicuous waterproof outer clothing in case you want to be seen, e.g. in hill country

Spare clothing

Drinks containers

Food container

Spare film

Camera

Small first aid pack

Ordnance Survey map in map case

Compass

Small stoppered containers for items collected

Torch with red filter

Battery

Whistle

Hand lens (×10)

Pocket knife

Notebook and pencils

Pouched belt for travelling light

The most valuable aid for the wildlife watcher is a good pair of binoculars. A wide range of choice is available and nowadays a good pair need not cost a fortune. When buying, test as many different pairs as possible – always stepping outside the shop to test them in daylight and over a range of distances.

The magnifying power and light-gathering ability of binoculars are given by numbers: 8×40, 7×50, 6×30 and so on. The first number is the magnification; the second is the diameter, in millimetres, of the objective lens and this governs the light-gathering capacity. To find the diameter of the exit pupil (the eyepiece lens) you divide the large number by the smaller. The exit diameter of a 6×30 is therefore 5mm. Anything above 4mm will be adequate for wildlife-watching.

Higher magnifications may sound attractive but they are difficult to keep steady. For wildlife watching, $\times 7$ or $\times 8$ magnification, coupled with good light-gathering, gives the best results, so you could try 8×40 or 7×50, whichever suits your eyesight. Generally, the higher the magnification, the smaller is the angle of view although some binoculars are described as "wide-angle". Locating an animal with binoculars is not as easy as with the naked eye so a wide angle of view is very useful.

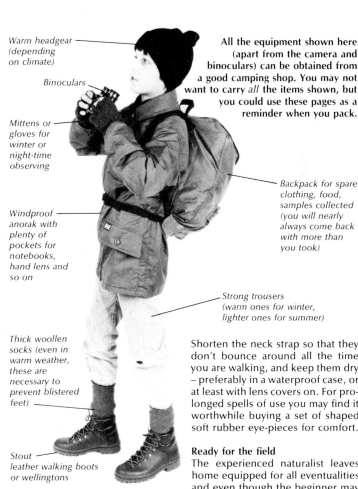

Warm headgear (depending on climate)

Binoculars

Mittens or gloves for winter or night-time observing

Windproof anorak with plenty of pockets for notebooks, hand lens and so on

Thick woollen socks (even in warm weather, these are necessary to prevent blistered feet)

Stout leather walking boots or wellingtons

Backpack for spare clothing, food, samples collected (you will nearly always come back with more than you took)

Strong trousers (warm ones for winter, lighter ones for summer)

All the equipment shown here (apart from the camera and binoculars) can be obtained from a good camping shop. You may not want to carry *all* the items shown, but you could use these pages as a reminder when you pack.

For ease of carrying, lightweight binoculars are preferable but when making a selection pay great attention to lens quality. Look at the straight edge of a building to check that there is no bending or distortion at the edge of the field of view. Also look for any coloured fringes around the image as these are signs of poor quality lenses and are best avoided.

To keep your binoculars in good condition don't knock or drop them.

Shorten the neck strap so that they don't bounce around all the time you are walking, and keep them dry – preferably in a waterproof case, or at least with lens covers on. For prolonged spells of use you may find it worthwhile buying a set of shaped soft rubber eye-pieces for comfort.

Ready for the field
The experienced naturalist leaves home equipped for all eventualities and even though the beginner may initially carry less specialized equipment, he or she should be able to stay warm and dry and able to enjoy wildlife-watching to the full. The safety rules are the same for everyone and apply whether you are in woodland, farmland, on the coast or in bleak hill country. Dress sensibly, tell someone where you are going and when you will be back, and take heed of weather forecasts and the advice of local people.

Keeping a record

A well-kept notebook is one of the naturalist's most valuable assets. The permanent record of observations made during each day in the field builds up into a fund of information over the years. Notes and sketches of unfamiliar or unusual species make it possible for these to be looked up later in reference books, so you need never be left wondering what that strange fungus or insect really was.

The book should be a convenient pocket size, about 10×15cm, and ruled with feint lines. Either hard-backed or spiral-bound books can be used though hardbacks do last longer. An elastic band will keep the pages flat even in gusty winds. Use a pencil for notes and always carry a couple of spares. (Choose brightly painted ones or wrap coloured adhesive tape round them to make them show up when dropped.)

Using a system

A notebook entry is only valuable if it is complete – that is, if it will enable you or someone else to return to exactly the same spot to repeat the observation, and if the details in it are sufficient to allow accurate identification of the species you have observed.

Always start with the date, the exact location, and the time of day and make a note of the weather conditions and the type of habitat you are in (see opposite). Then make notes and sketches of the animals and plants around you, remembering to include as much detail as possible about colour, size and shape and, in the case of an animal, what it was doing and how it behaved if it caught sight of you. If it is a bird, note any plumage patterns on your sketches: a simple bird shape will do – you don't have to be an artist. Try to estimate the size of the bird by comparing a "new" bird with a familiar one like a sparrow or a pigeon. A good way to measure an insect is to watch which leaf it was sitting on and then measure the leaf after the insect has flown off.

Comparing notes

Sharing your notes and sketches with members of your local wildlife society is a good way to learn more. And sometimes the significance of your experiences may surprise you. Some years ago, in Devon, I saw a woodcock "roding" – that is, flying in a special way that is always associated with nesting. It was only when I mentioned this sighting to another enthusiast that I learnt that woodcock had not been seen nesting in the county for many years. I had almost overlooked an important and interesting observation!

▶ The page opposite was copied from the author's own field notebook and shows how sketches and brief notes are used to record the animals observed. Some naturalists use a spiral-bound notebook in the field and then make a neat copy in a hardbacked book later. A useful tip: mark a centimetre scale on the back cover for making quick measurements of leaves, insects and so on.

You can also transfer the notes and sketches from your field notebook into a number of separate books – one for butterflies, one for wild flowers, another for birds and so on; or you could compile an illustrated diary for each year. In future years, your "collected works" will provide you with both entertainment and facts.

Location : Haldon Devon — Rough grazing and conifer woodland.
Date : JULY 16 1979 (am)
warm day, light w-sw wind, few clouds.

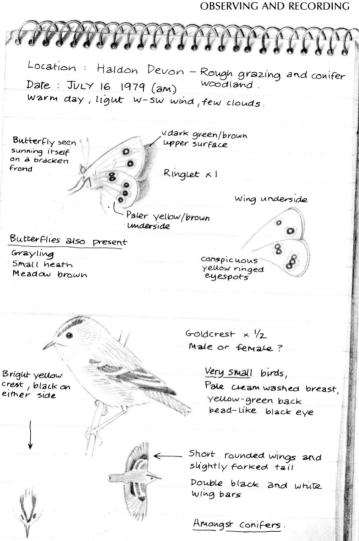

Butterfly seen sunning itself on a bracken frond

v.dark green/brown upper surface

Ringlet x1

Paler yellow/brown underside

wing underside

Butterflies also present
Grayling
Small heath
Meadow brown

conspicuous yellow ringed eyespots

Goldcrest x 1/2
Male or female?

Very small birds,
Pale cream washed breast,
yellow-green back
bead-like black eye

Bright yellow crest, black on either side

Short rounded wings and slightly forked tail

Double black and white wing bars

Amongst conifers.

Photographing wildlife

The quality of any photograph depends as much on the photographer's skill as on his or her equipment and it would be a mistake to think that good results can only be achieved with very expensive cameras and lenses. A simple camera is often much better for a beginner because it allows more time to concentrate on the subject and on composition.

The ideal system

Assuming that a photographer has some experience and wishes to improve his or her results, the best choice will be a 35mm single lens reflex (SLR) camera, preferably with through-the-lens (TTL) light metering. This type of camera will take a wide range of lenses from wide-angle to telephoto. Lenses are very important: the camera may take the picture but the lens produces the results; one or two really good lenses are much better value than a lot of poor quality ones.

For the nature photographer an

▲ A close-up lens, or a close-up adaptor for a standard lens, is ideal for insect and flower shots.

ideal system would include a standard lens (35mm), a "macro" lens (50 or 90mm) for close work, a medium telephoto (135mm) and perhaps a long telephoto (300 or 400mm).

With practice, telephoto lenses can be hand-held even at quite slow shutter speeds but there are limits and if you use too slow a speed you will almost certainly have problems with camera movement. As a guide, never use speeds slower than 1/125 sec. with a 135mm lens and nothing slower than 1/500 sec. with a long lens like a 400mm. If you need to use slower speeds, use a tripod.

Keeping it simple

Excellent photographs can also be taken with a simple non-reflex camera. These have just one lens, although on some models an inexpensive close-up lens can be screwed onto the front of the fixed

lens. By pre-setting the closest focussing distance on the lens, a projecting wire may be used to check the distance between camera and subject for close-up shots. Most of these cameras also have a "bright-line" frame inside the viewfinder so that you can see exactly what will appear in the photograph.

Practice makes perfect

Many beginners suffer from camera shake and this can often be cured by using a faster shutter speed or by resting the camera on something solid like a wall or tree.

Experience is the key to success and although the "pot luck" approach – going for a walk with camera at the ready – will bring its share of good results, it is worth remembering that professional wildlife and natural history photographers plan their shots in advance, working out their hide position, the position of the sun, distances and likely exposures, before they even think of taking the first shot.

▲ In protected moorland habitats, wild ponies have little fear of man and will often approach within easy range of a standard lens. (So, too, will safari park animals.)

▼ A long focal-length lens, such as a 135mm, 150mm or 200mm telephoto, will enable you to fill the picture area (the "frame") even when you are photographing quite small animals.

Sounds natural

Headphones for monitoring sound

Lesser spotted woodpecker

Parabolic reflector

Cassette recorder

▲ Using a parabolic reflector, clear recordings of birdsong can be made at ranges of up to 30 metres.

Exploring the world of natural sound can add a new dimension to watching wildlife. Animals can produce a surprising range of sounds, and by no means all of them are vocal. There is the rasping of a snail's tongue, the noisy feeding of a hungry hedgehog, the warning "thump" of a rabbit and the summer sounds of grasshoppers and crickets. The breeding season brings the clash of deer antlers and the wing-clapping displays of some birds. Add to these the countless calls and songs of birds, mammals and frogs and the possibilities are endless.

What you need

For quality recordings the ideal machine is a portable reel-to-reel tape recorder. These, however, are very expensive. But almost as good are some of the newer lightweight portable cassette recorders and here there is a wide range of choice.

When you are buying a recorder remember that you may have to carry it for long periods. Check it for weight (making sure that it has batteries in it at the time) and also find out how long one set of batteries will last. They can be an expensive item. The case should be strong, to give protection outdoors, and should give easy access to all the controls, even when being carried. The shoulder strap should be strongly sewn and fitted with a shoulder pad for comfort.

If possible use headphones to monitor the sound received by the microphone. Manual control of the recording level is preferable to automatic although today most portables are fully automatic.

Many recorders offer extras like

▲ **Keeping well hidden, a naturalist uses an imitation duck call to attract a flight of teal and mallard.**

Camouflage net

built-in microphones but these are not required for wildlife recording. Directional microphones can be very expensive but a parabolic reflector used with a standard "mike" will enable you to record at considerable distance from the subject. Here again, headphones are very useful as they let you check for background noises also collected by the reflector dish.

Play-back
Over the year you will be able to build up a library of bird calls and the more you play these back to yourself, the quicker and more reliable your field recognition will become. Always speak into the recorder at the end of a recording, giving the species, date, location and activity of the bird. If you record a bird but are unable to identify it, leave a gap on the tape. Later, you could "voice over" the details of the bird after checking its identity with another birdwatcher or by comparing it with pre-recorded tapes or records (see page 62).

Lore of the hunter
Many hunter's tricks can of course be used just as well by naturalists, and among them are various artificial calls that work by imitating the distress call of a prey species, the cry of a lost youngster, or by playing on the curiosity of many animals.

The clicking together of an old pair of antlers may attract a male deer to what he thinks is a rival in his territory. The imitated cry of an injured rabbit may bring fox or owl to the scene, and the fox may also come to a sucking sound made by the lips on the back of the hand.

Making a hide

Portable hide

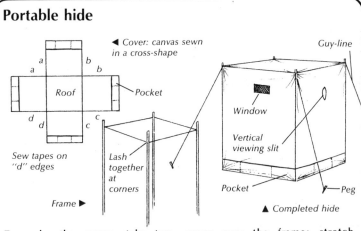

◀ Cover: canvas sewn in a cross-shape

Roof

Pocket

Sew tapes on "d" edges

Lash together at corners

Frame ▶

Guy-line

Window

Vertical viewing slit

Pocket

Peg

▲ Completed hide

To make the *cover*, take two 430×100cm lengths of plain or camouflage-dyed light canvas and sew them together as shown. Turn up 15cm on each of the four edges to form *pockets* on the inside. Then stitch together sides aa, bb and cc, leaving a small gap at each corner of the roof for the poles to stick through. Sew the fourth side (dd) part-way down and attach *tapes* at 10cm intervals (thus making the entrance). Make the *frame* from eight poles, ideally hazel or ash, lashed tightly with strong string. Place the cover over the frame; stretch *guy-lines* tightly from the top of the poles to *pegs* angled in the earth. (On hard ground tie them to rocks). Stones in the pockets will prevent any flapping.

Cut short, vertical *viewing slits* in the side walls. (Horizontal slits sag open and reveal your movements). Hold the slit open with a sharpened twig "pricked" into the fabric (see opposite). "*Windows*" of fine dark mesh may be added but cover them with flaps inside when not in use.

A hide is simply an artificial hiding place built in order to allow observation of wildlife at close quarters. It can be made of natural materials such as bales of hay or straw, branches, reeds, or rocks and pieces of turf, but these should be used only with the permission of the landowner. Old farm equipment or abandoned vehicles will also provide good cover. It is worth remembering that the motor car makes an excellent mobile hide if driven up slowly and quietly (and if the occupants remain still inside and don't keep getting in and out).

Most useful of all, however, is the portable hide favoured by birdwatchers. It is simple to make and erect, and very versatile. A hide can be used at any time of the year but is most valuable during the breeding season when animals, and birds in particular, are at their most vulner-

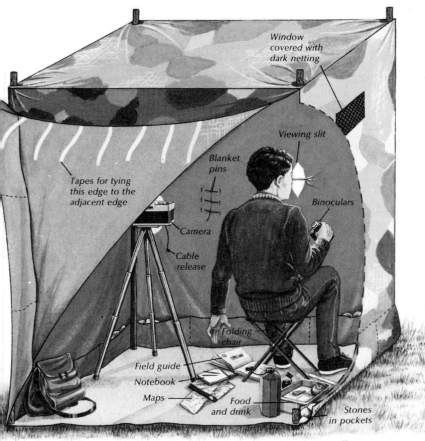

Window covered with dark netting

Viewing slit

Blanket pins

Tapes for tying this edge to the adjacent edge

Binoculars

Camera

Cable release

Folding chair

Field guide

Notebook

Maps

Food and drink

Stones in pockets

▲ As soon as you enter the hide, open all bags and wrappers, and set up all your equipment, to avoid noise later. Use blanket pins to close up gaps or slits that will not be needed, otherwise your movements may be seen.

able and nervous. The golden rule is that the hide should be introduced with the minimum of noise and disturbance. If a bird becomes unduly nervous, leave immediately. There is always another day.

It often causes less concern if you trick the bird into thinking you have gone away. Get someone to walk up to the hide with you and then ask them to walk away casually once you have slipped inside. A signal, such as a handkerchief hung outside the hide door, will tell your friend when to "collect" you again.

Outside the breeding season there is little danger of causing distress and a good place to start observing is at a pond or estuary where wildfowl or waders come to feed. There you can practise using the hide and also develop other skills like identifying birds in a mixed flock and estimating numbers.

ATTRACTING WILDLIFE

Baits, lights and lures

Once you have a good idea of what animals are living in your area – by locating their tracks, droppings, feeding signs, or other "clues" – it may well be possible to attract some of them into more open areas where you can get a better look at them. Many species live in well-hidden, inaccessible burrows (and with good reason) but a little cunning, skill, and fieldcraft may tempt them into full view.

The most obvious trick is to lay bait but for this to be successful the baiting must be carried out regularly, in the right place, and with the right bait for the particular animal sought.

Outfoxing the fox

Foxes will eat almost anything once they have been attracted to a regular baiting site. At the side of a well-used route, or "run", is usually a good place. Start by putting out a rabbit carcass (a road casualty will do perfectly), then introduce kitchen scraps like bread and fish. Foxes have, in fact, become so well adapted to living close to man that they are quite often seen in towns where they tend to put aside hunting in favour of scavenging in dustbins. But although the urban fox has become bold, his country relatives are still amongst the wariest of animals, and bait is best laid where it can be seen from a hide, preferably built well above ground in a tree or in an outbuilding.

Choosing the bait

Badgers, like foxes, will eat just about anything you offer but they

▲ *Good vibrations:* the secretive wall spider lives in a silk-lined hole but can often be tricked into the open by touching one of its radiating "trip wires" with a tuning fork! Like all spiders it is highly sensitive to vibration and so – mistaking the vibrations for the frantic struggles of a trapped fly – it dashes to the attack. Its retreat may be temporarily blocked by placing a twig across the hole.

are particulary attracted to a rich mixture made of peanuts and honey. Wood mice can be lured by a bait of seeds and cereals. Bank voles will come to chopped carrot and cereals, while field voles seem to prefer pieces of turnip and apple, a combination also relished by the water vole. In areas where squirrels are used to making raids on garden bird-tables their greed can easily be turned to advantage by putting out a mixture of nuts – oak, beech, hazel, chestnut and peanuts.

Scavenging birds can be attracted to a convenient part of an open field by a rabbit carcass, tethered to a stake to prevent it being carried away. Ideally, the bait should be

Silver Y

Brimstone

Common wainscot

Large yellow underwing

Broad-bordered yellow underwing

▲ *Night lures*: **by the time the last post has been painted with the sugar solution, the first has already attracted a selection of moths and more are arriving every minute. Try sugaring on warm nights between June and August. There are usually two spells of activity, the first about two hours after sunset and the second starting around one in the morning.**

placed near the edge of the field so that you can watch from the cover of a hedge or from a temporary hide made of straw bales, hurdles, or any other material familiar to these very suspicious birds.

Sweetness and light

Birds and mammals are not alone in falling for bait, and one very good way to observe moths is by "sugaring" a line of posts or trees. The main ingredients of the bait are something to give the mixture "body", a small amount of alcohol (to make the moths feel "drowsy"), and a powerful attractant. Many entomologists have their own favourite recipes but a simple one

would be: 4 tablespoons of black treacle, 2 tablespoons of beer, and 1 teaspoon of amyl acetate ("pear-drops"). The mixture should be kept in a tightly stoppered jar until required. On a warm, still, "muggy" summer's night, paint the mixture onto the posts in stripes about 2cm wide by 30cm long (see above).

An alternative method is to play on the attractiveness of light. Most purpose-built moth-traps are expensive, but for beginners a simple lure can be made from a white sheet laid on the ground beneath a powerful incandescent light like a "Tilley" lamp. Once the insects have been identified, they are released, preferably close to cover.

25

The garden sanctuary

Most hobbies and interests begin at home and wildlife watching need not be any different. Even in the midst of the city there is a host of birdlife to be seen; many species can be attracted by putting up nest-boxes; and by putting out suitable food in the hard winter months.

Our very tidy gardening habits are often not much help to insects, many of which need the nettles, michaelmas daisies, thistles, and dandelions that are all too often branded as weeds. For many insects such plants provide them with nectar, egg-laying sites, and food for their larvae. If your garden is big enough, try letting the bottom end, or a hidden corner, go back to the semi-wild state by planting wood-land and hedgerow plants that are native to this country, and some of the shrubs and perennials that are typical of the country cottage garden. The illustration shows some of the many other ways you can make a garden more attractive to wildlife.

Mammal life is less well adapted to urban life; however, in areas near parks, recreation grounds and public commons, and particularly in suburban areas where the open countryside is not too far away, it is quite possible for a garden to attract a number of mammal visitors – especially if the garden itself is safe and well supplied with plant and insect food and warm, dry places to make a home. You are not very likely to have a fox or badger take up residence but you may find that a pile of plant-pots and garden odds and ends has provided a safe, sheltered home for a hedgehog family or that frogs, toads or newts are breeding in your garden pond. And if they are, don't restock the pond with fish, which will compete for food. Our native amphibians need all the help they can get as natural ponds are drained, polluted, or filled up with domestic rubbish.

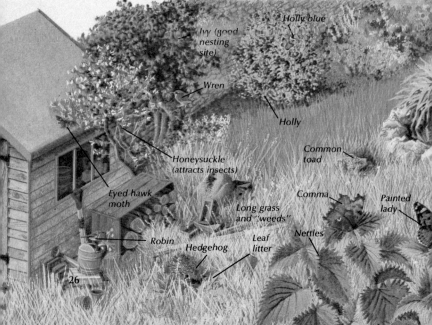

Holly blue

Ivy (good nesting site)

Wren

Holly

Honeysuckle (attracts insects)

Common toad

Eyed hawk moth

Comma

Painted lady

Robin

Long grass and "weeds"

Nettles

Hedgehog

Leaf litter

Woodpigeon

Trees and shrubs provide cover and nesting sites for birds

House sparrow

House martin

Chaffinch

Blackbird

Flowers to attract insects

Bird table: put out food in winter

Blue tit and nest-box

Thrush

Red admiral

Sallow

Buddleia (attracts butterflies)

Pond with water plants

Grey squirrel

Peacock butterfly

Common frog

Small tortoiseshell

Duke of Burgundy fritillary on primrose

Convolvulus hawk moth on tobacco plant (a garden flower)

Bee log (see page 11)

Cinnabar moth caterpillars on ragwort

27

WOODLAND WILDLIFE
The woodland mammals

Badgers

If there are badgers in your local woods they should not be too hard to find. Look first for the large sett, dug into a bank or the side of a slope. A large pile of excavated earth will spill down the slope from the main entrance and in many cases a furrow scraped in the earth will show where the busy animal has moved surplus soil well away from the entrance. The complex burrow may extend more than three metres below ground, with a number of separate chambers linked by tunnels. The badger is a wary and cunning animal and every sett will have a number of alternative entrances.

Then check for signs that the sett is in use. Fresh tracks and marks of digging are clear signs, especially in spring and summer. You may also find scratch marks on trees near the sett. To check which entrance is being used, lay a few small sticks across likely holes and call back the next day to see which have been moved. Alternatively, wind some adhesive tape, sticky side out, around an exposed root or firmly-planted stick, just inside the sett entrance. A passing badger will leave hairs on the tape.

Badgers are unusually clean and tidy animals so look around for the shallow latrine holes they make. Fresh droppings will confirm that the sett is occupied. Small piles of dry grass and bracken show that the

▶ **The features illustrated in this picture will enable you to identify a badger sett that is in use.**

old bedding has been cleared out and replaced by fresh dry grass. Well worn areas of ground may indicate where the young badgers play, and flattened vegetation will reveal paths that are in regular use.

Getting into position
Always choose your observation point in advance – and in daylight. Ideally you want a comfortable fork in a stout tree, about ten metres from the sett and two metres above ground so that any swirling wind is likely to carry your scent over the badger's head.

Badgers can be observed at almost any time of year. They do not hibernate though they are less active in winter. However, for those keen on seeing cubs, late April, May and June are the best months. Dress warmly and be in position by 9.00 pm. The animals will usually emerge soon after dark: if not, it is well worth waiting as they are sometimes slow to get moving. Often you will hear the most surprising noises for badgers are very vocal, grunting and

Main entrance

Adult badger

Excavated earth

Cubs at play

Old bedding

Path used by badgers

28

snorting and even making a sound like the clucking of a coot. After checking the air for danger, the family will usually stay near the sett for a short while before moving off to forage for food.

Hedgehogs

The hedgehog is one of the most appealing of our wild animals and also one of the easiest to watch. Although basically a nocturnal animal it differs from the badger in starting its activities usually around dusk instead of waiting for darkness. However, hedgehogs may also be seen in broad daylight – especially when a long dry spell is broken by a refreshing downpour and there are plenty of slugs and snails about.

Look for the animal's footprints in the earth bank at the side of a country road, or along the base of a hedge. Look also around farm buildings and haystacks as well as among the thick roots of woodland trees where the hedgehog likes to make its nest. Most of the day is spent fast asleep but once it is awake the hedgehog can cover quite a distance in its nightly wandering. If you get into position early, armed with your red-filtered torch, you will be able to follow its journey easily. Hedgehogs are tolerant creatures and so long as you walk softly it will not take fright.

In this way you can watch it feed, carefully noting what prey is taken and how the hedgehog deals with it. In addition to slugs and snails the very broad diet includes frogs, birds' eggs and nestlings, earthworms, mice and also a variety of berries, nuts and fruits.

The hedgehog is also an important predator on baby rabbits and this tough little hunter will tackle animals as large and fierce as rats with remarkable success. However, against foxes and badgers the hedgehog uses its own very special technique – rolling into a tight ball and presenting its attacker with a painful wall of sharp spines. The defensive prickles also serve another useful purpose. Hedgehogs are good climbers but are better going up than down: to descend, they roll into a ball and drop to the ground – the spines acting as an efficient shock-absorber so they bounce gently then unroll and scurry off unharmed.

Between three and seven blind, helpless young are born in a warm nest of moss and leaves, usually between May and July. A second litter may be born in early autumn but for them it is a race against time: they must put on plenty of weight if they are to be able to hibernate safely through the winter.

▼ If you don't crowd a hedgehog too much, you may be able to follow it for miles as it hunts for food.

ratch marks

Rear exit of badger sett

Hedgehog's nest of moss and leaves

Badger's latrine

Hedgehog

Red squirrel, grey squirrel

In Britain we have the native red squirrel, which is also found all over Europe, and the slightly bigger grey squirrel, introduced from America during the last century. Disease had reduced the number of red squirrels even before the grey ones arrived, and when the number of squirrels eventually grew again, the grey squirrel became the more common in most areas.

The best time of year to watch these delightful little animals is in the late summer and early part of autumn as they search for food among the leaf litter and collect nuts and beech mast from the trees. As winter approaches and the trees lose their dense covering of leaves the squirrels are much easier to watch as they scamper along the branches with amazing agility, sometimes leaping over three metres from one tree to the next. Their sharp claws provide a sure grip and the bushy tail acts as a balancing aid.

The red squirrel prefers conifer forest although it also inhabits deciduous woodlands – especially beechwoods. The grey prefers beech, oak and hazel woods although it too may be found in conifers. Both make a spherical nest known as a "drey" (see above). It is made of woven twigs, lined with

Red squirrel and drey

moss, leaves and strips of bark. The squirrel usually makes one large main winter nest, in which the young are born, and also a number of smaller ones which serve as temporary sleeping quarters.

The main foods are acorns, pine seeds, beech mast and hazelnuts, but squirrels will also take wild cherries, the bark and young shoots of pine trees, and birds' eggs and nestlings. The marks left by the squirrel on nut shells and cones are very distinctive (see below) and most wildlife watchers will very quickly learn to recognize them. The most certain clue to the presence of squirrels is the carpet of feeding litter spread on the ground beneath a favourite tree.

Adult squirrel

Young squirrel

Spruce cone has a typically ragged look and a pointed or frayed end

◀ Signs of feeding by squirrels on hazelnuts and a spruce cone. The squirrel gnaws a notch across the end of a hazelnut then puts its lower incisors into the crack and levers the shell open. Young animals take time to learn the trick and their teeth-marks are not nearly as neat as the adults'.

Wood mouse, shrew

The wood mouse is also called the long-tailed field mouse, and with good reason for it is equally at home in woodland, field, hedgerow or garden – anywhere, in fact, that provides plenty of ground cover.

Its large black eyes give an immediate clue to the fact that it is mainly a nocturnal animal, and watching one at night by the light of a red-filtered torch is certainly the most rewarding way to see one. However, the wood mouse can also be enticed out in daylight by laying bait beside one of its regular "runs". These pathways are often more like tunnels for the animal likes to keep under cover. It will, however, climb into a bush to get at a crop of ripe berries and will make surprising leaps, or bound away like a miniature kangaroo, if danger threatens.

The wood mouse feeds on all kinds of berries, nuts, acorns and seeds and will also take worms, grubs, insects and spiders. Food is often hoarded away in large quantities in the mouse's underground burrows. The breeding nest is safely underground, but during the summer shallow burrows may be used, and nests may even be made above ground. Occasionally wood mice will raid gardens to feed on flower bulbs and crops of peas.

Wood mouse

Shrew

The **common shrew** is usually heard before it is seen – giving itself away by its shrill squeaking or chattering. It is one of our smallest mammals – forever on the move, and forever eating. It is active by day and by night, alternately sleeping and feeding around the clock.

The shrew's long twitching nose is perfect for snuffling among the leaf litter for insects and worms but it will quite often climb up grass stems and into bushes to catch insects. The winter is spent under the leaf litter but in summer the shrew is likely to be found out in fields and meadows and near hedgerows, and the ball-shaped nest of grass is often placed in the bank of a ditch or in the tangle of growth at the foot of a hedge.

▶ The tell-tale signs of a wood mouse that has been feeding. It is much neater than a squirrel, nibbling cones smooth and leaving no ragged fibres or rough scales. And instead of scattering the debris around, as a squirrel would, the mouse carries the cone away to a quiet feeding place.

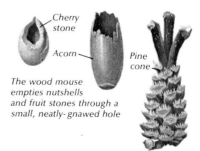

Cherry stone

Acorn

Pine cone

The wood mouse empties nutshells and fruit stones through a small, neatly-gnawed hole

A third-year roebuck moves quietly through the woodland browsing on leaves, shoots and shrubs, and grazing on grasses, fungi and a variety of forest floor plants. It is early spring and the buck is in velvet. Roe are active day and night but feed mainly in the early morning – often retiring into dense cover around midday.

Right forefoot

4cm

Deer

In addition to the native red deer and roe deer, several other species have been introduced into Britain. They include fallow deer, sika deer, muntjak and Chinese water deer. Deer parks offer the easiest way of observing these beautiful woodland animals but even where they are used to man's presence they are often still very shy.

Stalking requires skill and patience. The approach must be silent, always from the downwind side, and in dense cover as far as possible. (See page 40 for watching red deer in highland country and page 12 for alarm signals.) In many areas occupied by deer there are permanent viewing positions ("high-seats") placed in trees, so remember to ask about these when requesting permission to go on private land. One more important rule is that you should leave as carefully as you arrived. If deer are alarmed they will stay away from that area for days.

Each year the male deer replaces his antlers – his fighting weapons and the symbols of his strength and importance. The new antlers are at first covered with skin, known as "velvet" but as soon as they have hardened the velvet is "frayed" – that is, rubbed off by thrashing the antlers against a bush or sapling. The damage caused by fraying is one of the most dramatic animal signs. Roe deer also leave another characteristic sign when the buck marks his territory with scent from a gland on his forehead (see page 9).

In most species the old antlers are cast in the spring and the new ones frayed in late summer or early autumn. Roe deer are the odd ones out in casting in November and fraying in the spring. Cast-off antlers make fine trophies but unfortunately they are cast one at a time. Only where an animal has died might you find the two antlers together.

Other signs to watch for are the characteristic cloven hoof prints, the animals' droppings, and their regular pathways through the woodland and clearings. Roe deer are very fond of chasing around in circles, especially in the rut, so if you find a circular path – often round a tree or isolated rock – you have found a promising observation point.

Pipistrelle bat

Entice a bat into close range by flicking a tiny pebble into its path as it swoops after insects. Detecting the pebble by echo-location, the bat will often dive to investigate – sometimes taking a couple of turns round the falling object before deciding that it is not a tasty meal after all. A bat may even swoop at an angler's cast.

Bats

Bats are fascinating creatures to watch, for despite the "horror film" image they have been given, they are very clean animals, quite harmless, and also unique among mammals in being the only mammal group to have mastered the art of flying.

The bat's wing is supported by the very long finger bones, not the arm bones as might be expected, and its flight is far more agile than that of even the most acrobatic bird. At full speed it can virtually stop, spin round, somersault and flash away in another direction as it hunts in the gathering dusk for night-flying moths and other insects. Prey are seized in the mouth or scooped up with the wing or the membrane between the back legs, and then transferred to the mouth. The bat's remarkable echo-location system enables it to home in on its prey with deadly accuracy and to fly swiftly among trees in complete darkness without hitting anything.

During the day bats retire to their roosts in caves, hollow trees, and buildings. Church belfries and old warehouses are "traditional" roosts but quite recently bats were found to have taken up residence in the cavity walls of the houses on a new estate. The best place to watch for bats is near a suitable roosting place, often given away by the animals' droppings. The bats usually stream out to hunt as darkness falls. All British species are now protected.

▲ Greater horseshoe bats hang upside down in clusters from the roof of a cave. Hibernation is from October until March or April, but in a very cold spring it may continue into May or even into June.

Watching at night

This observer has prepared a safe and comfortable place in a tree in order to watch woodland animals at night. While you don't need a high seat to see a mouse, you need to be well clear of the ground in order to avoid detection by other animals such as badgers. The scent of this observer will be carried above the heads of any ground-dwelling animals.

Try night-watching in other well-populated habitats such as dense hedgerows, using the techniques of locating, attracting and observing wildlife explained elsewhere in this book.

Permanent padded seat

Wood mouse attracted by bait

Hedgehog

Watching wildlife at night is a rewarding pastime, not at all sinister as some people's imagination would have them believe. Sitting quite still, it is remarkable how much can be heard and, once your eyes have become accustomed to the darkness, how much can be seen as well.

Torches should be used very sparingly at night as they will ruin your night vision for several minutes after they have been switched off. You can, however, modify an ordinary torch for night use by fixing a red filter (or a piece of red cellophane) over the lens. Most animals seem completely unaware of red light.

Creatures of the night

Many of our native animals are nocturnal by habit, emerging under cover of darkness to hunt or forage for food. The badger, for instance, is truly nocturnal, rarely emerging until well after sunset whereas the hedgehog is already busy at dusk (see pages 28–9). The common dormouse actively forages at night for food, often climbing trees on woodland edges to do so, but this charming little creature is extremely difficult to see. However, some small rodents, such as wood mice, can be attracted by bait.

Much easier to spot are the many invertebrates that are active at night: moths being the most varied in shape and colour (see page 25). Other invertebrates, such as slugs, woodlice and centipedes, need to avoid losing moisture during the day, and are therefore less active

Bats leaving roost in old mill

Nightjar hawking after moths

Barn owl hunting rodents

Badger emerging from wood

Fox with rabbit

than during the normally cooler, damper nights. They can be seen in the leaf litter, or even climbing the bark of the trees in search of food.

In contrast there are very few birds abroad at night. The haunting hoot of a tawny owl and the piercing screech of a barn owl are sounds to remember, but even more thrilling is the sight of an owl twisting and turning among the trees or along the hedgerows in its hunting flight. In heathland and woodland clearings in summer a really fortunate observer may even see a nightjar.

Dusk is also the time to watch and listen to bats, for although the noises they make in order to locate their prey are too high-pitched for us to hear, their alarm signals *can* be picked up by the human ear.

Safety First

Being out at night obviously requires care, good sense, and preparation – so follow the code of safe conduct.

1 Never go out alone.
2 Make sure that someone at home knows *exactly* where you are going, and when you intend returning.
3 Get to know the study area very well in daylight. It is all too easy to become disorientated in darkness.
4 Wrap up well, including a hat and gloves, and take a hot drink and food with you.
5 Carry a whistle in addition to a torch in case of emergency.

Exploring an oak tree

Look at an old oak tree. From a distance it is a magnificent sight with its massive trunk dividing again and again into the gnarled and twisted branches of its huge spreading canopy.

Look again, and you begin to see signs of life. Birds fly in and out carrying nesting materials, or food for their young. A squirrel runs along a branch and disappears from sight, startling a great spotted woodpecker that had been exploring a patch of rotten wood.

Closer still and you can see ants, beetles, spiders and centipedes running about over the rough surface of the bark while greenfly, caterpillars and an assortment of strange-looking bugs fly, jump and wriggle among the leaves. Some of these insects chew the leaves, some pierce them to suck the juices inside, while others are there mainly to lay their eggs. Some are hunters, some the hunted – this single tree is like a forest in its own right.

Borers and miners

Out of sight beneath the bark the borers are at work. Several kinds of beetle and their larvae, and even the caterpillars of certain moths, live inside the trunk and branches of the living tree. Some make shallow tunnels just below the bark while others tunnel deep into the heart of the tree causing a great deal of damage. Leaves too are attacked by "miners". The larvae of weevils, sawflies and tiny moths known as "micros" tunnel inside the leaf, feeding on the soft green flesh without breaking through the tough outer skin.

Other insects cause galls to form on leaves, buds, twigs and even on roots below ground. The gall is a mass of plant tissue, usually in the shape of a ball or plate, that forms as a reaction to insect eggs or grubs. They do no lasting harm to the tree but provide shelter and a neat food-store for the insects.

Plants without soil

There are plants, too, that grow high up on the tree rather than on the ground. They are called "epiphytes" and range from the green powdery lichen that commonly covers the trunk, to a dozen different mosses and a wide variety of ferns, herbs and other flowering plants. These are all green plants, able to manufacture their food from sunlight and from the nutrients absorbed through their roots. Also common on oak trees are various kinds of fungi. Unlike the green plants, these have no chlorophyll of their own and so they live as "parasites" – taking their food from the tree (and sometimes causing its death) or else living off rotten wood or the decaying leaves carpeting the ground below.

Things to do

A single tree offers a huge range of fascinating projects (see opposite for some suggestions).

You can also make a collection of epiphytes and then try to work out how they came to be in the tree. Were they carried by the wind, or by birds perhaps? Another area to inspect is the soil around the roots of an oak. Here you may find large grubs of insects, which could be kept for observation in a subterrarium (see page 39).

Tree studies make ideal group projects so why not involve your friends, or become a member of one of the many naturalists' clubs?

▼ Collecting and hatching galls

Dozens of gall-producing insects live on oak trees and although the insects themselves are tiny and hard to find, the galls they cause are often brightly coloured or at least large enough to be seen easily. They can be kept in a dry, well-ventilated jar until the adult flies emerge.

▼ Bark and gallery rubbings

If you see a piece of loose bark, lift it carefully to see if anything has made a home beneath it. (And replace it just as carefully when you have finished.) If you find the galleries of an oak bark beetle, try making a rubbing with paper and a crayon or soft pencil. You can also make bark rubbings.

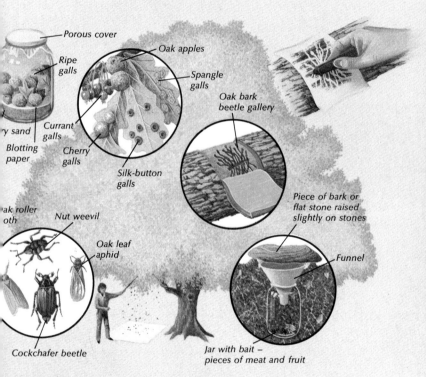

Porous cover

Ripe galls

y sand

Blotting paper

Currant galls

Cherry galls

Oak apples

Spangle galls

Silk-button galls

Oak bark beetle gallery

Piece of bark or flat stone raised slightly on stones

ak roller oth

Nut weevil

Oak leaf aphid

Funnel

Cockchafer beetle

Jar with bait — pieces of meat and fruit

▲ Tree-life survey

Place a white sheet beneath a low branch and then beat or shake the branch to dislodge the creatures living in it. Sort the galls, grubs, caterpillars and so on into groups and count them, identifying as many as you can. Make sketches of the animal life for your records.

▲ Leaf litter surveys

Cut the spout from a wide funnel, place it in the neck of a large jar containing bait, and bury them in the soil under a tree as shown. Insects will slip into the jar and be trapped. Check your trap often to avoid starving the insects, and remove the trap (or seal the top) in rainy weather

The forest floor

If you look closely at the many different plants that make up a wood, you will find that what looks at first like an untidy jumble of vegetation is, in fact, quite neatly organized. Usually it is possible to pick out four distinct layers, one above the other.

The upper layer (or *canopy*) is formed by the trees themselves. They support a wealth of animal life, and plant life too, but just as importantly they affect everything beneath them by shading the ground, protecting it from wind and excessive frost, and by shedding a carpet of leaves. Below the canopy comes the *shrub layer*, sometimes very dense, sometimes quite thin. In some broadleaved woods, for example, the tangle of brambles and hornbeam, hawthorn and hazel provides cover for a variety of birds and an ideal place for spiders to spin their webs.

Closer to the ground lies a rich *herb layer* made up of grasses and nettles and familiar woodland flowers. And last of all comes the *ground layer*, consisting of mosses and other ground-hugging plants, and also the *leaf litter*, slowly decomposing and adding to the soil.

Woodland low-life

Woodland leaf litter tends to be overlooked by many naturalists and yet in broadleaved woods it teems with animal life of all kinds. No sooner does a leaf fall to the ground than it begins the process of breakdown that will eventually return all its useful nutrients and fibre to the soil.

Woodlice, millipedes and a great variety of worms are among the plant feeders that help break down the leaf material, while that same thick layer of debris gives cover to hunting insects like the centipedes, hunting spiders and numerous beetles. Many of the ground beetles are glossy black with a dramatic green, bronze or purple sheen, and some have stink glands in their defensive armory. Scurrying about in the leaf litter, under flakes of bark, and among mossy ground vegetation, they hunt for worms, grubs and other insects. However, even more fearsome than the beetles are some of their own larvae. The tiger beetle larva, for example, is a strange creature that lives in the mouth of a vertical burrow in the soil. When some unfortunate insect strays too close, the larva pounces and drags its prey underground.

Many of the smaller creatures of the forest floor are well worth a close look and specimens can be collected quite easily with simple traps. Pieces of tree bark or hollowed-out grapefruit halves can be placed on the ground, but best of all is a jar sunk in the soil below a slippery plastic funnel placed with its edge level with the ground (see page 37).

A few minutes' digging with a small trowel, especially around the base of a large tree, will usually produce a variety of large larvae and earthworms, many of which can be kept in a subterrarium like the one shown opposite.

Habitats to study

Even a short walk along a woodland path is likely to provide a number of interesting micro-habitats – the name used for small areas in which, for various reasons, conditions are not the same as in the overall habitat.

Inside a wood you could make a

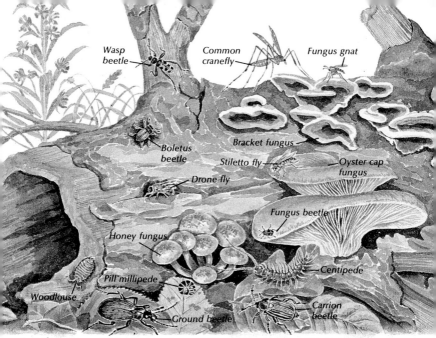

Wasp beetle

Common cranefly

Fungus gnat

Boletus beetle

Bracket fungus

Stiletto fly

Oyster cap fungus

Drone fly

Honey fungus

Fungus beetle

Pill millipede

Centipede

Woodlouse

Ground beetle

Carrion beetle

▲ In the ten years that went by between falling to the ground and finally rotting away to powder, this large branch section provided food, breeding sites and shelter to dozens of animal and plant species.

detailed study, preferably repeated at intervals, of a decaying log. All the insects and plants growing on and around the log should be noted but samples should not be removed and any pieces of log that are moved should be replaced with great care exactly as they were.

A similar study can be made of any small mammal or bird carcass and this will provide an opportunity to watch the activities of the various sexton beetles in addition to ground beetles and many flies. Nothing is wasted. The flesh disappears very quickly but even bone and feather will rot away in a few months.

Even a pile of animal droppings will soon accumulate a number of interesting insects, in addition to the birds who prey on the dung-beetles and flies.

Subterrarium

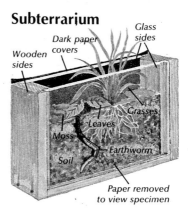

Glass sides

Dark paper covers

Wooden sides

Grasses

Leaves

Moss

Earthworm

Soil

Paper removed to view specimen

▲ The subterrarium is usually kept dark by the black paper covers but these can be removed to observe the specimen and to take photographs or make sketches.

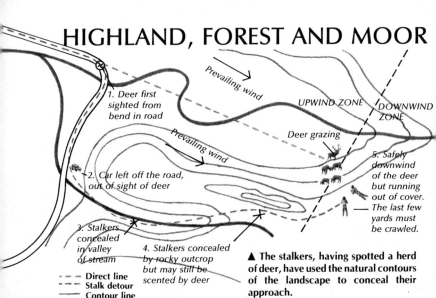

1. Deer first sighted from bend in road

Prevailing wind

UPWIND ZONE / DOWNWIND ZONE

Deer grazing

2. Car left off the road, out of sight of deer

Prevailing wind

5. Safely downwind of the deer but running out of cover. The last few yards must be crawled.

3. Stalkers concealed in valley of stream

4. Stalkers concealed by rocky outcrop but may still be scented by deer

- - - Direct line
- - - Stalk detour
——— Contour line

▲ The stalkers, having spotted a herd of deer, have used the natural contours of the landscape to conceal their approach.

Red Deer

Although red deer may be seen in several parts of lowland Britain, the best place to watch them is in the dramatic hill country of the Scottish Highlands and Islands.

In winter, when there is little grazing to be had on the snow-covered hills, the deer will often come right down into the valleys, even to the roadside. Then, a car makes an effective hide if it is driven up slowly and quietly and if the occupants remain quiet and still.

In summer the deer roam far out onto the high moors and a long and careful stalk is necessary (see above). The deer has excellent vision, good hearing, and a very sensitive nose. If you see deer at the head of a glen and the wind is behind you, start your detour immediately – even if the animals are a couple of miles away. To avoid alerting them you will have to swing round in a wide arc, always keeping out of sight, until

your scent can no longer be carried to them on the breeze. Walk softly, without chattering, and avoid any patches of loose stones on the hillside. Always crawl forward and take a careful look *before* you go over the top of a rise. And whenever you are in view of the deer, watch them closely – especially the stag and leading hind. If they stop feeding or look towards you, freeze flat on the ground until they relax. Once frightened they will be off over the hill and may not settle again until they are miles away.

If possible, go out with an experienced stalker during September or early October when the rut is at its peak. The sight and sound of a big stag challenging potential rivals is an unforgettable experience, especially in the half-light of dusk or early morning (see page 12). At this time of year, look out also for muddy pools and boggy areas churned up and surrounded by hoof prints. The stags love to wallow and there can be few more dramatic sights than a stag heaving himself out of a wallow, dripping water and mud like some huge prehistoric beast.

Highland country is beautiful but should be treated with respect. Twenty minutes can see a change from warm sunshine to bitter winds or swirling mists, so dress warmly and keep an eye on the weather. If possible, go with an experienced person. It is safer by far, and you will learn much more. You may even be lucky enough to be shown the field signs of one of the rarer highland animals.

▲ This red squirrel was no match for the swift and agile marten.

Wild Cat

The northern Highlands are home to Britain's only wild member of the cat family. Larger and more powerfully built than the domestic cat, the wild cat lies up during the day in its lair among the hillside rocks but travels far and wide in its nightly hunts.

The cat preys on hares and rabbits, grouse and other birds, and may even take lambs and very young or weak deer calves. You will be lucky to see the cat itself but look out for prints – like those of a domestic cat but a little larger – and also for droppings. Like its domestic relative, the wild cat buries its droppings within its own territory, but around the edges of its territory it will leave them on top of rocks or grass tussocks to act as a warning to any other cat who wanders into the area.

Wild cats usually hunt alone, or occasionally in pairs – prowling the hillsides and mountain forests at dawn and dusk as they seek their prey. They are seldom seen but their harsh, unearthly cries are often heard as hunting cats call to each other.

Pine Marten

Even more rare is this large member of the weasel family. In ages past it was common throughout the woodlands of Britain but hunting and trapping greatly reduced its numbers. It is now found only in the hill country of northern England, Wales and Scotland, but in some areas it is thought to be on the increase.

The pine marten spends most of its time in the trees, preying on squirrels and birds, but it will also come down to the ground to hunt rats and mice and rabbits. Like all members of the stoat/weasel group it is a fearless and fearsome predator – quite capable of tackling prey larger than itself.

The marten is protected and on no account should it be disturbed. If you are lucky enough to see one, *don't* tell everyone around – but *do* let one of the main conservation organizations know of the sighting (see addresses later in this book).

GRASSLAND AND FARMLAND

Although grasslands may appear much the same at first glance they vary a great deal in the variety of plant life they support and the amount of food and cover they offer to animals.

Richest of all are old meadows and pasture lands and you can recognize these by the large number of anthills underfoot, skylarks overhead and by a general richness of wild flowers and their associated insects – bees, flies, butterflies and grasshoppers. Mature limestone and chalk grasslands are drier and have their own characteristic plants and insects.

Along with natural grassland we must also consider farmland. Fields of turnips offer a feast to animals as different as badgers, voles and deer, while grass crops like wheat, oats and barley attract mice and voles and countless seed-eating birds – often to the great annoyace of the farmer. The boundaries between different types of farmland, often marked by hedges, ditches or small clusters of trees, also provide opportunities for wildlife communities to develop and flourish (see pages 48–9).

The grassland mammals

Wild rabbit

One of our most familiar animals is the rabbit, and yet only 30 years ago it was almost wiped out by the virus disease myxomatosis. In some areas 99 per cent of the wild rabbits died but they are now recovering.

Where the population is still low, the rabbits often live above ground and this makes them difficult to watch at close range, but where the numbers are larger the rabbits live in the more familiar warrens.

Rabbits are most active at dawn and dusk and the best way to watch them is from a nearby tree, or better still from a hide built on stilts right in the middle of the warren. You could also use a wall or hedge as cover but if possible get above their level – they have a very good sense of smell.

To stop them wandering off to feed, place small heaps of rabbit pellets near the burrows. You can buy them from any pet shop and the wild

▼ A large rabbit warren is an ideal place to study animal behaviour.

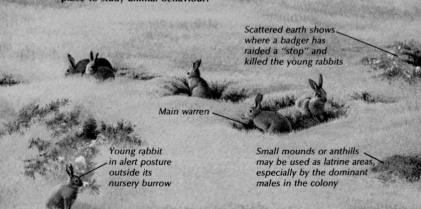

Scattered earth shows where a badger has raided a "stop" and killed the young rabbits

Main warren

Young rabbit in alert posture outside its nursery burrow

Small mounds or anthills may be used as latrine areas, especially by the dominant males in the colony

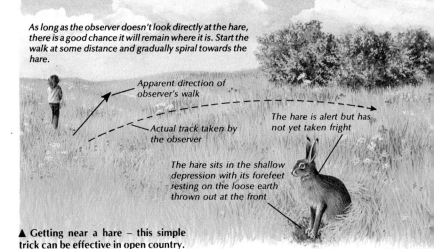

As long as the observer doesn't look directly at the hare, there is a good chance it will remain where it is. Start the walk at some distance and gradually spiral towards the hare.

Apparent direction of observer's walk

The hare is alert but has not yet taken fright

Actual track taken by the observer

The hare sits in the shallow depression with its forefeet resting on the loose earth thrown out at the front

▲ **Getting near a hare – this simple trick can be effective in open country.**

rabbits love them. A rabbit warren offers plenty of scope for studying behaviour, especially in March, April and May – the height of the breeding season. Try to work out the family groups within the colony, and the order of rank within each family. Look also for the nursery burrow, called a "stop", that the female digs some distance away from the main warren. If you have a well-placed observation position you will be able to watch the doe visiting the stop to feed her young, and later you will see the youngsters make their first excursions into the outside world.

Brown hare

Unlike the rabbit, the hare is a solitary animal for much of the time although males (jacks) and females (does) may be seen together throughout the spring breeding season.

Hares are creatures of habit, always crossing hedges and walls at the same places and sticking to favourite tracks. Careful watching and noting of footprints will tell you the best place to put your tree-seat

or build your hide.

If you see a hare in open ground you can try another tactic. Walk along steadily, in full view but at an angle to the hare and without looking directly at it. If you keep altering your line towards the animal you will walk in a spiral round it but you will always appear to be walking past, minding your own business. Like all field tricks it doesn't always work but sometimes it will bring you surprisingly close.

The lowland (brown) hare rests in a shallow depression called a form, usually well hidden among long grass, but the closely related Scottish mountain, or arctic, hare makes more use of natural cover and often hides in crevices among rocks. Like the stoat, the Scottish hare turns white in winter.

In either case watch for the remarkable behaviour of the doe as she approaches or leaves her young. To break her tell-tale scent trail she will make sudden enormous leaps at right-angles to her direction of travel, sometimes springing onto a bank or wall, or out into a patch of marshy ground to kill the scent.

43

An area of farmland containing a mixture of cornfields and pasture land, damp meadow and marshland, provides the perfect setting in which to look for our smaller mammal species. Moles inhabit the well-drained pastures, the field vole (or field mouse) likes damp grassland areas, while the agile little harvest mouse prefers tall vegetation like the long-stemmed marsh grasses, and crops such as wheat.

Mole

Although few of us ever see a mole we are all familiar with its field signs – the conspicuous mounds of earth that are dotted around arable land and pasture.

For its size the mole must be among the strongest of animals, able to burrow through the soil at a fast rate in its ceaseless hunt for earthworms, leather-jackets, wire-worms and other insect larvae. It burns up energy so fast that it must eat right round the clock, alternating bouts of frantic activity with short rest periods spent in its nest chamber. This is usually just below ground level beneath a large mound of earth, 30cm high and more than 1m in diameter. The nest itself is a ball of grass and leaves.

The extensive network of shallow burrows can often be seen as ridges running along the surface, while the mole's secondary system of deeper hunting burrows is revealed by the small piles of earth pushed to the surface all over the field (see opposite).

A mole can be studied in captivity for a short time but it needs a large earth-filled box, a supply of water, and a huge amount of food. If his food stock runs out late in the evening he probably will not live until morning so you *must* make sure he is well supplied.

Moles can be caught during ploughing, or when root crops are being lifted, but you must be quick – they can "dive" out of sight in a few seconds. To avoid bites, hold him firmly round the body, just behind the front legs.

Field vole or field mouse

Field voles are common in meadowland and damp grassland but may also be found in woodland margins, parks and gardens. They feed mainly on the green stems of grasses and their feeding signs are very characteristic (see opposite). A little path is often worn around the base of a grass tuft or bunch of rushes. The stems are bitten off near the ground and pieces carried a short distance away, where they are then gnawed.

In severe winters field voles may cause damage to young plantation conifers and to apple trees by gnawing off the bark in a ring around the base of the trunk. These tiny animals also do a good deal of damage even in the summer months but at this time of year the vole does not eat the bark but instead gnaws away the thin growth layer of the tree which is uncovered as the bark is stripped off.

The field vole has a system of underground burrows, some of which are used as food stores, but the burrows are also connected to a maze of little surface pathways hidden under the grass. These "runs" are completely covered and can usually only be seen if you part the grass over them (see opposite). The

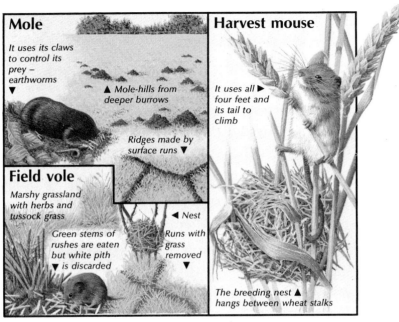

Mole

It uses its claws to control its prey – earthworms ▼

▲ *Mole-hills from deeper burrows*

Ridges made by surface runs ▼

Field vole

Marshy grassland with herbs and tussock grass

◄ *Nest*

Green stems of rushes are eaten but white pith ▼ *is discarded*

Runs with grass removed ▼

Harvest mouse

It uses all ► *four feet and its tail to climb*

The breeding nest ▲ *hangs between wheat stalks*

female makes her little domed nest of woven grass just off one of the runs, sometimes under the additional cover of a hedgerow root or fallen branch.

Harvest mouse

This remarkable little acrobat is the smallest British mammal apart from the pygmy shrew and in its physical adaptations and behaviour it is perfectly suited to life amongst tall grassy vegetation.

It usually feeds by climbing the grass stem, stealing the seeds from the "ear" at the top, then carrying them down to ground level to eat them. At various times of the year the mouse will also take berries, growing plant shoots, and a variety of grubs and larvae. Like many small animals it uses up its energy very quickly and therefore the day is taken up with alternating periods of feeding and resting.

The nest is a sphere of interwoven grass leaves, plaited together after being stripped lengthwise into fine strands. It is made from the living grass and is green when fresh but usually fades to brown in the autumn. The breeding nest (shown above) is larger and more strongly made than the rather loosely-woven sleeping nest.

In close-up the harvest mouse is fascinating. Its tiny feet, both front and back, are adapted for grasping, and the last 2cm of the tail is prehensile – that is, it can be coiled round a stem to act almost as a fifth "hand".

Only a high seat will enable you to escape detection by the returning adult as it circles round the den, checking it from every side

Wind direction

Cubs love to play, especially in the early morning and early evening, but they soon learn to be wary of intruders

▲ **Not even the hardest tree seat can spoil the thrill of watching a family of wild foxes.**

Red fox

Unlike the badger, who uses the same home throughout the year, the dog fox and vixen come together only during the breeding season. From July until March the animals live alone, and their movements are quite unpredictable. The pair mate in winter and the cubs are born in April or May in a den or "earth" excavated in the side of a bank. Very often the fox will take over a rabbit burrow and enlarge it, and on several occasions foxes have been seen sharing the same burrow complex with a badger family.

The fox's territory usually covers a variety of habitats including farmland with hedges and ditches, open country, scrubland and some woodland. If you make careful notes each time a fox is seen or heard in the area a pattern will soon emerge and this will give a clear idea of the animal's territory and favourite routes. Early in the spring you can look for signs of an occupied den and a number of

unmistakable field signs will tell you whether or not a burrow is occupied by foxes. Firstly there is the strong smell – quite unlike that of any other animal you are likely to meet. Secondly the fox is a messy housekeeper and the ground around the entrance will be littered with the remains of its prey – feathers, bones and bits of fur – and with droppings. These can be quite interesting in themselves. In summer, foxes eat a lot of berries and their droppings become stained with the juices, but when animal prey is the main food the high proportion of bone in the food makes the droppings white or grey.

The best fox-watching period is May to June when the youngsters are tied to the earth, usually guarded by the vixen while the dog is away hunting. As the cubs get older the parents leave them for short spells and then you can often creep up to quite close range – as long as you approach carefully from downwind.

If the parents are away you can climb into a tree nearby and wait for their return. And here you will see just how wary the adult fox is. Instead of making a direct approach to the den, the returning fox will circle round, checking the wind for any sign of trouble and finally coming in from directly down-wind. That is why it is important to get well above ground. Once the vixen scents danger she will bark a warning to her cubs to get underground, and she will move the family to a new home at the very first opportunity.

Stoats and weasels

If ever you see a rabbit frozen to the spot, or running along a woodland path looking dazed, freeze absolutely still at once. You may then see one of nature's most ruthless hunters in action. The glazed look is fright, and following close behind, in no great hurry, will be the rippling, bounding shape of a stoat. Before many more minutes have passed the stoat will pounce, putting the rabbit out of its misery with one quick bite at the back of the head.

Stoats and weasels are among the most elusive and difficult animals to watch. They are small, slender, very quick in their movements and very agile so you must make the very best of every chance meeting. If you come across a stoat crossing a country road, stop and remain quite still. The animal will vanish into cover in a flash – but will then reveal one of its most delightful characteristics. Within a few seconds, curiosity will get the better of it and its head will pop up as it takes a long hard look at *you* with its piercing black eyes before vanishing again from sight.

▲ A stoat in its summer coat: the tip of its tail is always black, unlike that of the weasel.

Like most predatory mammals, stoats and weasels love to chase and wrestle, especially when young, and if you are lucky enough to spot a breeding den in a hole in a wall, or in a hollow tree or an old rabbit burrow, then careful watching will bring huge rewards.

The weasel is like a small version of the stoat, very tiny, and slender enough to follow mice right into their holes. Like its larger relative it is a ferocious hunter and because it burns up so much energy it must eat about one-third of its own weight in food each day. Despite its small size – no more than 22cm long with a 6cm tail – the weasel will tackle animals as large as rabbits and, much more impressively, full-grown rats. Apart from the difference in size, and slight differences in colouring, the main difference between the two animals shows itself in winter when, in the northern part of its range, the stoat turns silvery white but for the jet black tip to its tail. In this form it is known as ermine.

Life of the hedgerow

Like a vast lattice criss-crossing the countryside, spanning valleys and encircling moors and mountains, the hedge is, surprisingly, mainly a man-made structure. Varying greatly in size and shape, the vast majority of hedges were planted to form field boundaries and enclosures although a few are the sad remains of former woodland margins. These woodland relics can often be identified by combinations of typical woodland plants – dog's mercury, primrose, bluebell and hazel among them.

As more and more woodland disappears from the countryside, the hedges become increasingly important as places of shelter and as foraging grounds for many animals. But even the hedges are under constant pressure. Modern agriculture demands large open fields, not a patchwork of small ones, and recent years have seen thousands of miles of mature hedgerow ripped out in the name of efficiency.

Robin in threat posture

Songposts

▲ The robin, a familiar hedgerow bird, becomes noisy and aggressive at the start of the breeding season. The males broadcast their claims to their chosen territory by singing loudly from well-placed songposts.

See if you can identify these songposts on several visits to the same area, marking them on a map.

Residents and visitors

In addition to the small mammals like the shrew, bank vole and wood mouse, the hedge provides nesting and feeding niches for a great many birds from resident blackbirds, finches and dunnocks to visiting fieldfares and redwings. The insect and spider population is enormous, with beetles, butterflies, moths, bugs, crickets and flies of all kinds providing another rich source of food for predatory birds and mammals. Reptiles and amphibians also make their homes in the banks at the foot of the hedge.

Other animals use the hedge as a routeway or as temporary cover. A sparrowhawk, for example, will often fly fast and low close to a hedge or woodland edge, remaining hidden until it suddenly swerves into view to pounce on some unsuspecting small bird. Songbirds make use of convenient posts and trees in a hedge for warning off rivals. Many butterflies also use the still air in the lee of a hedge when migrating across country, following the line of the hedge whenever it lies roughly in the right direction.

Studies along a hedgerow

The age of a hedge can be estimated from the number of different species of shrub and tree it contains. Pace out a length of 30 metres, and count the species. Allowing 100

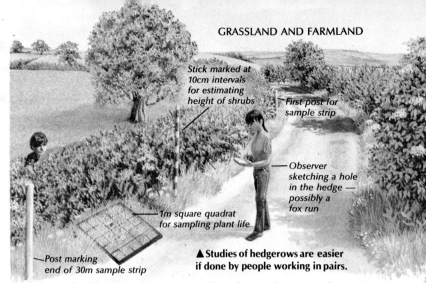

Stick marked at 10cm intervals for estimating height of shrubs

First post for sample strip

Observer sketching a hole in the hedge — possibly a fox run

1m square quadrat for sampling plant life

Post marking end of 30m sample strip

▲ Studies of hedgerows are easier if done by people working in pairs.

years for each different species you see, you can then estimate roughly the age of the hedge, by taking an average over several sample sections. Five or six hundred years is by no means rare. At the same time, you could measure all the shrubs in the hedge and identify them. Use a post to judge their height (see above).

The vegetation on both sides of the hedge is also worth studying; you could compare the hedgerow vegetation found on one type of soil with that found on another type. Rather than laboriously count every specimen and every species along the whole hedgerow, you can use a "sampling" technique which cuts down the area of study to one square metre.

To do this, you need to make a grid, or "quadrat" as shown on this page. It consists of a wooden frame, one metre square, divided up into smaller segments by pieces of cotton or string. Your record sheet should be drawn up showing the same number of small segments.

Place the quadrat at random on areas whose vegetation you wish to study, then mark on your record sheet the position and number of different plants that fall within the quadrat. If, for example, daisies occur in ten of the small segments in one random search, but in only two segments in another area, this fact should be noted: it may point to a different type of vegetation in the second area. A sample taken in this way on a wet area will yield quite a different plant "profile" from one taken in a dry area: what other factors might influence vegetation?

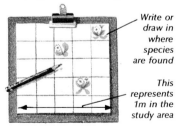

Write or draw in where species are found

This represents 1m in the study area

Divide your record sheet into segments, just like the quadrat.

Spiderwatch

Folklore and tradition have not been kind to spiders. Like sharks and snakes they are widely disliked and even feared by many people, and yet this seems rather unfair for not only are spiders very useful but they are also among the most fascinating of creatures. One of our leading experts has estimated that a single acre of undisturbed meadow may have a spider population of well over two million. Think of how many more flies there would be without these busy and efficient predators.

Some spiders are adapted to life in wet conditions, others to dry: some can tolerate low temperatures while others must keep warm: some hunt by day while others are active in the hours of darkness. The web-spinners feed mainly on flying insects, or make snares to catch running or creeping insects, but the free-ranging hunters use various chase and ambush methods to capture their prey.

Looking for spiders

Their generally dull colouring and very small size make spiders quite difficult to see, but many can be located by looking for their delicate and intricate snares.

The best time to look for web-makers is early in the morning with the dew still glistening, or after a light shower of rain. Move forward slowly, if possible towards the sun so that the webs catch the light and so that your shadow does not fall across the web. Spiders have poor eyesight except at extremely close range, but a sudden shadow spells danger – often from an attacking bird – and is the signal to dash for cover.

When you get close to a web, check carefully for long radiating strands. These threads are sometimes quite long and if you break one the spider will be on the alert. To lure a spider into the open, try the tuning fork trick (page 24) or select a very fine feathery grass stem and touch it against the web with a trembling movement. The spider makes up for its limited vision by being extremely sensitive to vibration and most species dash out to investigate a possible "catch".

To sample spider populations you can lay a sheet below a small bush and give it a good shake, or make up a strong version of a butterfly net and sweep it across long grass in a meadow or marsh. Best of all read about the different types (some are described on the opposite page) because once you know their habits, the sooner you will be able to discover for yourself the secrets of their remarkable life-styles.

Garden (or cross) spider —

Questions to ask

Locate a garden spider and watch it closely for as long as possible. What insects does it catch? How does it deal with them? Which does it eat, and how many? Does it reject any? Where does it lie in wait?

Make a tear in the web and watch how the spider repairs it. Which parts of the web does the spider walk on? Are they different from the "snare" regions? Look for a spider beginning a new web and see if you can work out the sequence of movements as the web takes shape.

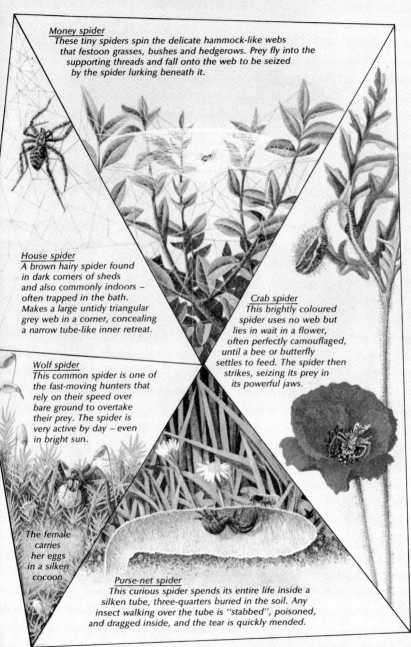

Money spider
These tiny spiders spin the delicate hammock-like webs that festoon grasses, bushes and hedgerows. Prey fly into the supporting threads and fall onto the web to be seized by the spider lurking beneath it.

House spider
A brown hairy spider found in dark corners of sheds and also commonly indoors – often trapped in the bath. Makes a large untidy triangular grey web in a corner, concealing a narrow tube-like inner retreat.

Crab spider
This brightly coloured spider uses no web but lies in wait in a flower, often perfectly camouflaged, until a bee or butterfly settles to feed. The spider then strikes, seizing its prey in its powerful jaws.

Wolf spider
This common spider is one of the fast-moving hunters that rely on their speed over bare ground to overtake their prey. The spider is very active by day – even in bright sun.

The female carries her eggs in a silken cocoon

Purse-net spider
This curious spider spends its entire life inside a silken tube, three-quarters buried in the soil. Any insect walking over the tube is "stabbed", poisoned, and dragged inside, and the tear is quickly mended.

Amphibians and reptiles

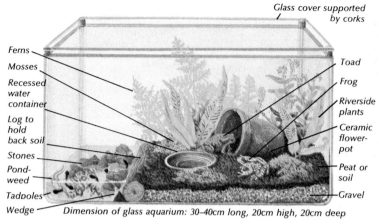

Glass cover supported by corks

Ferns
Mosses
Recessed water container
Log to hold back soil
Stones
Pond-weed
Tadpoles
Wedge

Toad
Frog
Riverside plants
Ceramic flower-pot
Peat or soil
Gravel

Dimension of glass aquarium: 30–40cm long, 20cm high, 20cm deep

Amphibians

Frogs and toads are tied to water during part of their life cycle but are land-dwelling for a large part of the time. In the breeding season (mainly February and March or later for the common frog; mainly March and April for the common toad), frogs and toads congregate at ponds and lakes to mate and spawn. They can be found at night by torch-light if you walk quietly around a suitable spot.

Both these amphibians call to their mates before breeding, so on a warm, damp night, at the appropriate time of year, you could explore local ponds for the animals or their spawn. A tape recorder with a directional microphone (see page 20) will enable you to record their croakings.

Because their skin has a coating of mucus, and also because it damages easily, frogs and toads should be handled as little as possible. If you want to transfer them to a container, catch them with a net.

▲ Vivarium for a common frog or toad. It is best to keep one of these amphibians for not more than six months (from about April), and then to return it to the place where you found it.

A small amount of spawn can be introduced into such a vivarium. If you keep only an adult, however, the "pond" area is not essential – keep the contents moist by spraying regularly with a plant mister. Site the vivarium in a cool but light spot, avoiding intense sunlight.

At home, you can observe common species in a suitable vivarium made from a glass aquarium, as shown above. Provide the frog or toad with sufficient food (live insects, worms or maggots from an angling shop), and let it take what it needs. Feed young tadpoles on algae found on waterweeds, and small aquatic life found in pond-water. Older tadpoles can be fed on small worms and tubifex (from an angling shop). Return the young frogs or toads to the pond where you

Tracks and signs of snakes are ▶ very difficult to detect, and they leave virtually no droppings. However, you may find an empty skin. Snakes shed their skin several times during the year as they grow larger. The process of shedding the old skin is known as "sloughing".

The best time to look for sloughed-off skins is April, when there isn't too much vegetation to hide them. Look around gorse or bramble bushes – the adder rubs itself on thorny sticks to help loosen the skin. If you find one, notice how even the covering for the eyes comes off with the rest of the skin.

Male adder sloughing skin. He starts at the head and the skin is slowly turned inside out until shed.

Sloughed-off adder skin – an attractive trophy for a collector

found the spawn.

Newts are less easy to find than frogs or toads. However, you may spot an adult at night during the late spring or early summer near a pond, with the aid of a torch.

Lizards

The most commonly-found lizard in this country is the legless slow-worm. It can be distinguished from a snake by the regular size of the scales on its back and stomach (snakes have scales of varying sizes on their body). The slow-worm can often be found under pieces of old metal in gardens, or along disused railway banks.

Many other species of lizard occur in continental Europe and some can be attracted by bait put down in a place where they have already been seen: for some reason, they seem to favour bananas!

Lizards, if handled, should be touched only very gently, and *never* held by the tail: in many species it will come away at the slightest pull.

Snakes

In Britain we have only one poisonous snake – the adder (see above). Its bite is very rarely fatal but it is very painful. In continental Europe there are many more venomous snakes, but, like the adder, none of them will do any harm if they are left alone and observed quietly from a safe distance. A snake sunning itself on a rock is to be watched, admired, photographed: a beautiful animal both at rest and in motion, but one that should not be handled.

Adders are more easily found than our other native snakes – the grass snake and the smooth snake – and April or May is the best time to look. Choose a clear, still, sunny morning that is not too hot. Search in quiet spots on heathland, downland, hedgerows or woodland edges. Walk very softly (snakes can detect footfall easily; however, they will not be able to hear you talk). Carefully check sunny banks that face south or east. Listen, too, for the sound of a snake slithering away into the undergrowth.

LIFE OF THE RIVER

The riverbank mammals

Otter

Sadly, otters are now among our less common animals and any observer who manages to watch one will have scored quite a success. They occur mainly in areas that are relatively undisturbed by man – in quiet river valleys, in remote uplands dotted with streams and tarns, and in the wet lowlands of eastern England. They are nocturnal by habit and may sometimes be caught in the headlights of a car while out hunting, but most "observations" consist of their tracks and other signs.

Otters are great travellers and often make long journeys both by river and across country. They are found from the coast, hunting along the shore for shallow-water fishes, crabs and shellfish, right up to the rushing headwaters of mountain streams. In highland regions otters will often cross miles of bleak upland in order to move from one river valley to another. Although beautifully adapted to life in the water, they can move surprisingly quickly on land, usually with a supple bounding movement that leaves a very distinctive trail (especially on snow-covered ground).

During the day the otter lies up in thick vegetation, often in a reed-bed but occasionally on a low branch or in the crown of a pollarded willow. These temporary resting places are called "hovers". Only when the otter bitch has cubs with her does she use anything like a permanent home. This takes the form of a den called a "holt", dug out of the river bank and usually overhung by vegetation or hidden among the roots of a tree. The entrance is often underwater.

Among the clearest signs that otters are present are their droppings – called "spraints". These are black and rather slimy when fresh, with a strong oily smell. They are often placed on prominent stones, tree stumps or grassy tussocks so that they act as territory markers. The otter's footprint is distinctive although the web between the toes shows clearly only in snow or soft mud. Like many mammals, otters are playful and they seem very fond of

◄ Otter cubs love to wrestle and chase each other

Fish bones and scales, or crab shells, mark an otter's feeding place ▼

◄ An otter's "slide"

A swimming otter leaves a characteristic V-shaped wake ▼

sliding. Grassy or earth banks on favourite routes often show the deep furrow mark of an otter slide, (see below, opposite) and these "toboggan runs" are especially common when there is snow.

Water vole

The smaller riverside mammals are much easier to watch than the secretive otter, particularly as they are active during the day.

The water vole can be found on most stretches of quiet, slow-running river or stream and also along canal banks. These appealing little animals prefer tall riverside banks with plenty of lush vegetation in which they can forage for food, and a careful search will often reveal small patches of vegetation where the plant stems have been neatly bitten off. The water vole's riverbank burrow is easy to identify because the vegetation has usually been grazed for several centimetres all round the entrance.

Your first sign of a water vole is quite likely to be a sound rather than a sight of the animal – a loud "plop" as it makes a dive into the safety of the water having heard you

approaching. If this happens, find a comfortable position in the shade, against a tree or bank that will hide your outline, and wait quietly. The vole will usually reappear within a few minutes and carry on unconcerned.

Water shrew

Like the water vole, the water shrew is short-sighted and is easy to watch as long as you make no loud noises. It is extremely agile in the water, chasing bugs and beetles on the surface, sometimes jumping out of the water to snap up a flying insect, then diving down to walk along the river bed looking for caddis-fly larvae and other small creatures. Its thick fur is dark grey or brown above and silver-grey underneath and holds a lot of air so the animal has a characteristic silvery appearance under water. The water shrew does not hibernate, and in winter a lucky observer may see one hunting under the ice on a frozen stream or pond. The burrow is quite shallow although a deeper hole, lined with soft moss, is usually made as a nursery for the young during the summer breeding season.

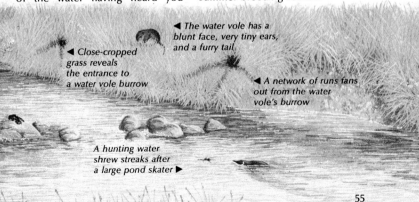

◀ The water vole has a blunt face, very tiny ears, and a furry tail

◀ Close-cropped grass reveals the entrance to a water vole burrow

◀ A network of runs fans out from the water vole's burrow

A hunting water shrew streaks after a large pond skater ▶

55

Freshwater life

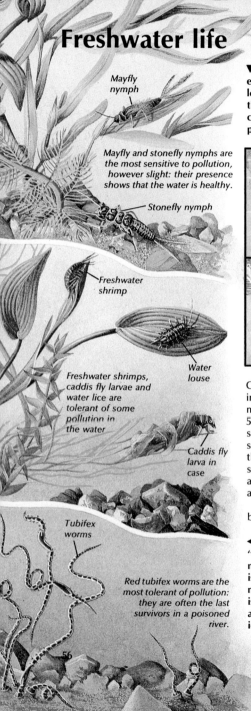

Mayfly nymph

Mayfly and stonefly nymphs are the most sensitive to pollution, however slight: their presence shows that the water is healthy.

Stonefly nymph

Freshwater shrimp

Water louse

Freshwater shrimps, caddis fly larvae and water lice are tolerant of some pollution in the water

Caddis fly larva in case

Tubifex worms

Red tubifex worms are the most tolerant of pollution: they are often the last survivors in a poisoned river.

▼ Polarizing sunglasses make an enormous difference when you are looking at a water surface. Almost all the surface glare is removed, giving a clear view of the bed of the stream or pond.

Countless plants, fishes and invertebrates, as well as the mammals already mentioned (on pages 54–5) depend on fresh water for their survival. A patient riverside or pool-side observer will need to look for these creatures and the clues or signs of their presence not only in and on the water, but also in the air above it and along the banks.

Most freshwater areas are rich in birdlife – ducks, geese, kingfishers,

◀ Look for these animals (known as "indicators") in fresh water to esti-mate how polluted or clean the water is. If they are all present, including members of the first group, the water is very clean. Some rivers, however, are so full of waste and harmful chem-icals that nothing can live in them.

A simple home-made underwater viewer cuts out the glare of reflected sunlight and the distortion caused by ripples. Remove the top and bottom of a large tin and fix clear plastic film over one end. Place the "window" end in the water and look through the open end, if necessary using your hands as blinkers to cut out light from the sides.

herons, coots and moorhens being the most easily found. There are also those fascinating animals whose lives are spent partly in the water and partly out. Many go through egg and nymph stages in the water before emerging to spend their adult lives at the surface or flying above it.

Where to look

The richest habitats for freshwater life are the lower reaches and estuaries of the river, for here the broad, meandering stretches of water lie between banks crowded with vegetation, and the slow-moving water contains a varied and plentiful supply of food. Higher up the river, in the hills where it has its source, the rushing mountain torrent holds very few species: the trout (above left) has the oxygen-rich waters almost to itself.

If you are lucky enough to be near a lowland stream that is unpolluted, the technique shown above for looking under the water surface will prove useful. Don't, however, try this on the banks of a big river – you might fall in.

The main pollutants of freshwater are chemical wastes from industrial processes, untreated sewage, and hot water from power stations, and the most affected areas are the larger, slow-moving rivers.

Certain animals act as indicators of the purity of the water (see illustrations on the opposite page), so you could gain an impression of how clean your local river or stream really is by searching for these species.

57

SHORE LIFE

The narrow strip of land we call the seashore is one of the most fascinating habitats on earth. It can vary in just a few miles from gently sloping sandy beaches backed by sand dunes or saltmarshes, to huge areas of mud-flats that are swamped by the sea at every tide, or to jagged rocks reaching out into the sea from the foot of towering cliffs.

Each of these habitats is home to a vast number of highly specialized animals and plants, many of which are not found in any inland habitat. On the shore we can see a succession of "life zones", each of which harbours animals that are adapted to the particular conditions of that environment. All the seashore zones are compressed into a band often as little as 100 metres wide.

The outer edges of this band are marked by the low-water line, beyond which the shore is permanently under water, and the high-water mark where the land really begins. One of the most interesting studies is to take a strip, say a metre wide, from above the high-water mark to beyond the low-water mark and to examine all the different life-forms it contains – finding out just how each one is suited to life in its own part of the beach.

Beachcombing
Above the high-water mark is the strand line – a stretch of seaweed thrown up by the tides; rubbish; empty shells of molluscs and crustaceans (such as crabs); driftwood; bones and egg cases of various fishes (such as the dogfish), and other such collectable items. Within this beachcomber's paradise are the living creatures that benefit from any available food sources – tiny sand-

Observer inside a seaweed-draped canvas bag

▲ **Rock pools, sand dunes and sandy beaches are among the habitats that the naturalist can explore.**

hoppers, flies, and larger animals like gulls and turnstones that pick off tiny shellfish, or worms and other organisms that are clinging to the weed or bits of wood.

This is one of the more accessible areas of the beach to explore for wildlife, along with rock pools, for these are self-contained mini-habitats within the larger area of the shore

Birdwatching
For millions of wading birds and wildfowl the great river estuaries provide an unfailing source of food – especially in winter when huge flocks of birds travel south from their northern breeding grounds to over-winter in warmer parts of the world.

Their activities are governed by the tides and for birdwatchers the best time of day is usually about two hours before high tide. As the tide surges up the estuary, worms and all kinds of molluscs emerge from their burrows to feed on the rich supply of food carried in the water, and as the tide rises higher the birds become

Use a net to catch marine creatures in a rock pool – but don't let your shadow fall on the surface

A quadrat makes it easy to compare sample areas from different dunes

more and more concentrated in a narrow band.

The birdwatcher can also find plenty of species to study on a rocky or sandy beach, but in these habitats every trick of self-concealment is needed to get close to the birds. On rocky shores, make careful use of the cover available from the rocks themselves, but on open, sandy beaches, you may need to resort to the method shown above and lie in wait, hidden in a camouflaged canvas bag that disguises your tell-tale shape. This method obviously requires patience, as well as care in getting into position without causing too much disturbance. Check out the beach you have chosen for footprints of birds before you decide on the best spot.

Behind the beach

Areas of sand dunes and shingle will often be used by gulls and terns for their simple scraped nests, but dune areas in particular may also contain familiar heath birds such as skylarks and wheatears. When you are exploring dunes, watch out for well-camouflaged eggs that are easily crushed underfoot, and try to avoid known breeding areas during the nesting season – it may disturb the birds.

Sand dunes and saltmarshes offer far more than just birdlife. Here again the specialists thrive and the plant kingdom and insect worlds provide a wealth of interest for the naturalist, and opportunities for making field observations.

A dune survey of plant life can also be carried out using a quadrat (see page 49). What species are present? How are the plants adapted to their constantly shifting environment? For a longer-term project choose a recently-formed dune (one on which relatively few species have become established) and plot its progress over the months or years.

Cliffs

Millions of seabirds lay their eggs on precarious cliff-ledges, safe from ground predators and free from disturbance by man. For similar reasons, grey seals will favour caves and beaches hidden away at the foot

59

of steep cliffs or on remote rocky islands. The best way to spot these birds and mammals is therefore from a boat, accompanied by some-one with local knowledge of the animals' haunts.

The heath-like habitat along the cliff top is home to many interesting wild flowers and insects (including butterflies), and here too the naturalist may find reptiles, birds such as the stonechat, and even larger mammals like the fox.

Play it safe
The coast is no place for taking chances. Never walk far out on mud-flats unless you know the area very well. At the very best you may lose your wellingtons in the sticky mud. By the same token it is foolish to go out on a low rocky headland without keeping a careful watch on the incoming tide – and on your route back to the beach. Finally, never try to look over a cliff: cliff-top winds swirl in all directions, and if you *are* near enough to look over the edge it is more than likely that you will be standing on an overhang – and this could give way under your weight at any moment.

Coast watch

Every year thousands of tons of litter – plastic bottles, drinks cans, bits of metal, plastic and wood – are washed ashore on our beaches. This mountain of rubbish gets little publicity compared with the outcry that follows an oil spill, and yet it grows day by day, piled up by each incom-ing tide. It is unpleasant to look at, it causes injuries, threatens wildlife and occasionally it can pose a very serious threat to health. More than once, rusting or punctured contain-ers have come ashore leaking dangerous chemicals.

Problems must be properly understood before they can be sol-ved. And that is where you can help; by joining in the **National Shoreline Litter and Refuse Survey**. It is quite straightforward. You can do it alone, with your family, or through your school. It can be done occasionally, during weekend or holiday visits to the coast or, if you live near the sea, you can make a regular survey of a chosen study area. Every single sur-vey form filled in provides valuable information, and hard facts are the best weapons in the fight against pollution of the sea.

How to join in
If you want to find out more, write to the Keep Britain Tidy Group, Bostel House, 37 West Street, Brighton BN1 2RE. (Special information sheets are available for school teachers and youth leaders.)

WHERE TO FIND OUT MORE

Zoos, museums and nature trails

Before setting out to watch animals in the wild it is worth visiting a zoo or a wildlife park. There, wary animals like deer can be studied at leisure and you will be able to learn the differences in size, colour and antler shape of the different species. Later, if you catch a brief glimpse of a deer melting into cover in a woodland glade, you may still be able to identify it with confidence. Remember also to look for hoofprints in the earth of the deer's enclosure. They are reliable field signs and worth memorizing.

The casual visitors
Not all the animals in a zoo are kept in captivity. Attracted by an easy source of food, and perhaps by the presence of so many other animals, many wild birds frequent the enclosures, gardens and ponds of the zoo. Many become surprisingly tame and woodpigeons, coots and moorhens can be approached quite easily – even though in the wild they are among the most wary of creatures. Even so, remember to make a slow casual approach.

Local museums
Make good use of your local museum. A few days spent looking at the animal specimens will make it so much easier to recognize animals in the country. Summer and winter plumage of birds and the different colour phases of juvenile and adult birds can also be studied, and specimens have one great advantage over book illustrations – you can learn to appreciate the actual size of the animal.

The staff are usually only too keen to help and encourage you and local museums, like local libraries, are often a good place to find out about local clubs and societies. Once you have become interested in watching wildlife, joining a club is one of the best ways of getting the most out of it because you will be learning from others all the time.

Nature trails and reserves
The National Trust, County Naturalist Trusts, the RSPB and the main National Parks all have trails and walks in various parts of the country. The trails are well laid out, often with display boards and signs pointing out interesting animal and plant features, and they provide a useful "half-way" stage between books and museums, and doing fieldwork on your own. Many of them offer guided tours and these are a marvellous way to learn about a new area or to improve your plant, bird or insect recognition with a knowledgeable guide to help you.

Many of the reserves set aside for the protection of birdlife have permanent hides from which you can observe in comfort without causing any disturbance. They are often placed so as to overlook places where birds gather in large numbers. While admission is free to most reserves it is also very often controlled in order to protect the habitat or to avoid disturbing the wildlife residents. Some reserves are "closed", and admittance is by permit only, so remember to write to the warden, or telephone his office, *before* you make your visit.

Books, clubs and societies

Books

A **Field Guide to the Mammals of Britain and Europe** by F. H. Van Den Brink (Collins). Also in that series, **Birds of Britain and Europe**, **Wild Flowers**, **Trees**, **Insects**, **Mushrooms**, etc. and the very useful **Guide to Animal Tracks and Signs** by Bang and Dahlstrom.

Finding and Identifying Mammals in Britain by G. B. Corbet (BMNH).

David Stephen's Guide to Watching Wildlife (Collins).

For younger readers the **Usborne Spotters Guides** provide simple, clear field-guide information.

First Guide to Cameras and Photographs by P. Hawksby (Usborne).

A Wildlife Photographers' Code of Practice (RSPB).

The Oxford Book of Insects by J. Burton (OUP).

Collecting from Nature by T. J. Jennings (Wheaton).

A Handbook for Naturalists Mark Seaward (Constable).

Wild Life in the Garden by T. J. Jennings (Pergamon).

The Amateur Naturalist's Handbook by V. Brown (Faber).

Field Natural History by Alfred Leutscher (Bell).

Studying Insects by R. L. Ford (Warne).

A range of cassette recordings of British bird-songs, and video recordings of birdlife, is available from the **Royal Society for the Protection of Birds** (see below).

Clubs and societies

Please remember to enclose a self-addressed stamped envelope whenever you write to a society asking for information.

County Naturalists' Trust. You can get the address of your local Trust from the Royal Society for Nature Conservation, 22 The Green, Nettleham, Lincoln LN2 2NR. They will also give you information about the **WATCH** club — the junior branch of the Nature Conservation Trusts. **WATCH** has its own magazine, projects and local groups.

County or Local Natural History Societies. You can get the address of your local Society from CoEnCo, Zoological Gardens, Regents Park, London NW1. They plan programmes of talks and outings each year.

The Field Studies Council, Information Office, Preston Montford, Montford Bridge, Shrewsbury SY4 1HW. Runs outdoor courses in different aspects of natural history including wild flowers, held at its nine residential centres in Britain.

The Young Zoologists' Club, Zoological Gardens, Regents Park, London NW1.

Young Ornithologists' Club and the **RSPB** (Royal Society for the Protection of Birds), The Lodge, Sandy, Bedfordshire.

The Mammal Society. For information about youth membership write to: Ms Lenton, 5 St. Stephens Court, Bath, Avon.

The Amateur Entomologists' Society has younger members as well as adults. Write to: 355 Hounslow Road, Hanworth, Feltham, Middlesex.

The Wildfowl Trust, like the RSPB, owns several reserves. For details about junior membership write to: Membership Secretary, The Wildfowl Trust, Slimbridge, Gloucestershire.

INDEX